In Search of Leaders

In Search of Leaders

Hilarie Owen

JOHN WILEY & SONS, LTD

Chichester • New York • Weinheim • Brisbane • Singapore • Toronto

Other Wiley Editorial Offices

John Wiley & Sons, Inc., 605 Third Avenue,
New York, NY 10158-0012, USA

WILEY-VCH Verlag GmbH, Pappelallee 3,
D-69469 Weinheim, Germany

Jacaranda Wiley Ltd, 33 Park Road, Milton,
Queensland 4064, Australia

John Wiley & Sons (Asia) Pte Ltd, 2 Clementi Loop #02-01,
Jin Xing Distripark, Singapore 129809

John Wiley & Sons (Canada) Ltd, 22 Worcester Road,
Rexdale, Ontario M9W 1L1, Canada

British Library Cataloguing in Publication Data

A catalogue record for this book is available from the British Library

ISBN 0-471-49197-7

Typeset in 11/15pt Goudy by Mayhew Typesetting, Rhayader, Powys
Printed and bound in Great Britain by Biddles Ltd, Guildford and King's Lynn
This book is printed on acid-free paper responsibly manufactured from sustainable forestry, in which
at least two trees are planted for each one used for paper production.

Contents

Preface

If the doors of perception were cleansed, everything would appear to man as it is, infinite.

For man has closed himself up till he sees all things thro' narrow chinks of his cavern.

William Blake, *The Marriage of Heaven and Hell*, A Memorable Fancy

'The ancient tradition . . .'

There is a widespread perception that our society is lacking leadership – whether in business, the City, politics, schools, the community or sport. As far back as 1988 Harvard Professor John Kotter was looking into the future when he wrote: 'It will be a world in which even the best "professional managers" are ineffective unless they can lead. . . . In general it will be a world in which the leadership factor will become increasingly important – for prosperity and even survival'.[1]

Also in 1988, the UK-based Ashridge Research Group wrote their report *Management for the Future*.[2] When looking into the future they wrote that organizations would be market driven, closer to customers and suppliers, flatter and more fluid in structure, and much faster moving. Above all, the report said, organizations would place unprecedented emphasis on people and talent as their most precious resource, on the need to develop individual potential, and on the need to draw out the commitment of all their people. They concluded that leadership would be a vital ingredient to the success of future organizations and that it would be needed at all levels.

In the summer of 1988, the *Sunday Times* had a headline 'Big chiefs fail the leadership test'.[3] The article showed the disappointment of managers in their chief executives. One of the reasons given in the article was the widely held assumption that all a business needs is one ultimate leader. This assumption of the 'great leader' is still with us today. For example, an 'Academy' for headteachers has been set up following a report from Chris Woodhead, the chief inspector of schools, that there were 2800 'incompetent' headteachers running English state schools.[4] Yet this will not address the issue of many teachers not wanting to take on headships because the role has become that of a general manager. Enticing people with incentives such as high salaries will only attract those individuals who are motivated by high salaries.

In 1996, the Centre for Research in Employment and Technology in Europe found that lack of leadership skills was the major issue for all employment sectors.[5] In 1997, research from the Industrial Society found the single largest issue concerning most organizations was developing leadership.[6] In 1999, Professor Nigel Nicholson of the London Business School remarked on the City in London: 'There is never a shortage of people who will fill leading positions, but there is a genuine shortage of leadership talent'.[7]

During the past decade we have seen more books on leadership in the 'business' section of bookshops than on any other subject. Fascination with the subject has grown remarkably. Most companies and public sector organizations are developing and running leadership programmes, with mixed results. Everywhere, a search for this elusive phenomenon is growing as we try to deal with a fast-changing world. In 1999, Watson Wyatt Worldwide identified leadership development as one of the top three concerns from 2143 companies in 23 countries.[8] There is in society at large a search for leaders.

A personal reflection

A couple of years ago I was running a team programme for a well-known financial company. Over coffee on the second day, two of the managers began to tell me that they felt there was something missing in their lives. Both were happy with their work and with their home and family life. At work they earned good salaries and enjoyed their present challenges. Both had recently become fathers and, although proud of their children, felt there was something more inside them which had not yet come to the surface. 'What could it be?', they wanted to know. Is this something you, the reader, can relate to?

Studying human beings, and in particular the concept we call 'leadership', has been a lifetime fascination. It began many years ago in a school in Wales where I was learning around 40 biographies of mainly men who had made an impact on the world during the first half of the twentieth century. This was O level history – my favourite subject. The biographies included Presidents Woodrow Wilson, Teddy and Franklin Roosevelt, Prime Ministers Lloyd George and Winston Churchill, Lenin, Stalin, de Gaulle, Mao Tse Tung and Adolf Hitler. Although only 16, I was fascinated by how events in people's lives sometimes had incredible results in the world.

Years later, as an undergraduate in political science, I was studying power on a global scale and the ways in which political 'leaders' used or abused this power. Along with politics, I was studying psychology in my first year and philosophy in my second. During those three years, I began to learn what it was to be 'human' and about the phenomenon we call 'leadership'. As a political scientist I had experience of research suggesting that how people vote seems to stem from how they perceive the world rather than what politicians say. There was also a strong element of people voting *against* something they did not want, rather than *for* something like a manifesto. People knew that they did not want any more Labour or Conservative parties, or Democratic or Republican parties, which gives parties 'in the middle' a difficulty unless voters see the two stronger parties as 'the same' or view the middle party as a viable alternative. It became clear that our perception of the world is reflected in our actions. This can be seen through many aspects of our lives.

A year after graduating, the business world became my focus for learning about leadership, both through further studies and through working in corporates, experiencing different bosses and colleagues.

During this time I was introduced to an organization called British Junior Chamber (BJC; nothing to do with Chambers of Commerce). The local group of 100 members was just beginning to accept women into its fold, and with a little resistance, I became Vice-President for Individual Development within a year.

BJC is part of a worldwide organization called Jaycees International. It is for professional people under 40 who want to develop their leadership skills. As well as being offered training opportunities, members can become active on committees that oversee events for the general public. I was on the committees for the Lord Mayor's Day and the Marathon, both in the city of Plymouth. I also set up and chaired a committee to address how to help people set up their own business – it was the early 1980s and 'enterprise' was taking off. Through these activities it was hoped we would become leaders in our community. It was challenging to do something very different to our working lives, while at the same time giving something to the community. It was as a member of BJC that I learned about John Adair's work in the field of leadership and the belief that leadership could be learned instead of being perceived as the sole preserve of a few. Today, his theory is out of date but at the time it was very good.

In 1990, I left the corporate world, where I had climbed up ladders and continued to learn, for a management consultancy which had very poor leadership within it. The managing director would tell Marks & Spencer how to run its business, but did not apply the same good advice to his own business, and many experienced being verbally abused by him. It was one of those 'toughening up' experiences most of us have and one which I know many of you will relate to. But it enabled me to learn how to become a consultant and opened doors to blue chip companies.

In 1991, I set up my own consultancy, and in 1993 began a two-year study of the RAF Red Arrows to establish how to develop high-performing teams. Doing the research felt like being an archaeologist who has to carefully dig away what time covers up to get to the information underneath. With patience and observation a picture emerged from which a model was developed. Since the success of publishing *Creating Top Flight Teams* my work has taken me worldwide, working with top teams throughout Europe, the USA and Middle East. Wherever I went, the same human issues emerged. Throughout I have continued to learn and study the phenomenon called 'leadership'.

A rainbow of knowledge

In Search of Leaders has been many years in the making. This time, the archaeology from the first book is joined by history, philosophy, psychology, business studies, politics, physics and economics to show that subjects need not be kept apart in separate boxes but can give a richness when interconnected in a bid to understand the world.

One of the founders of understanding modern leadership is James McGregor Burns, who won a Pulitzer prize for his book entitled Leadership. He wrote: 'No central concept of leadership has yet emerged, in part because scholars have worked in separate disciplines in pursuit of different and often unrelated questions and problems'.[9] Here, the attempt is to discover leadership without falling into the trap of seeing a subject through only one pair of coloured spectacles – but instead through a rainbow of colours that are related and connected.

In addition, this book is an attempt not only to stimulate your rational, deductive and reasoning process, which the left side of the brain thrives on, but also to stimulate the intuitive, creative and imaginative right side of your brain through story telling. Therefore there are stories throughout which you can pass on to others who want to understand leadership. Stories are easier to remember and we all enjoy relating to them.

Hilarie Owen

Acknowledgements

The ideas presented in this book took over fifteen years to mature and present. Throughout I have been inspired by both individual writers and individuals expressing their leadership. There are too many to record all of them here, but I would like to mention those who have greatly influenced my work and my life.

There have been many writers, individuals and thinkers who have left their mark on me. These include:

Mary Parker Follett
James MacGregor Burns
Warren Bennis
John Gardner
Judy Rosener
Robert Greenleaf
Margaret Wheatley
Sally Helgesen
Joseph Jaworski
Tom Peters
Lao-tzu
Francis Hesselbein
Peter Senge
Carl Jung
Abraham Zaleznik
David Bohm

Abraham Maslow
Daniel Goleman
James Kouzes and Barry Posner
Thoman Kuhn
Oprah Winfrey
Bryan Magee
Albert Einstein
William Blake
Vaclav Havel
Nelson Mandela
Ben Okri
William Shakespeare
W. Edwards Deming
Charles Handy
Fritjof Capra
Kahlil Gibran

In particular, I would like to thank Adrian Thurley and Simon Meade for their time, Claire Plimmer, my editor, for her support and patience and John Moseley, development editor at Wiley. I would also like to thank the two teachers who planted the seeds that led to this work: Dr Dave Dawson and Dr Mike Burgess.

Last but not least, I would like to dedicate this book to my son Darren and to all young people, into whose hands we pass this world.

Introduction

$\mathcal{L}$ eadership is a daunting subject and much has been written about it. The writers who stand out are Mary Parker Follett, James MacGregor Burns and Warren Bennis, all of whom began as political scientists before moving across to the business schools. In similar footsteps, I would like to continue their work and that of others in trying to understand leadership. Most of the books on the subject have focused on business 'leaders', i.e. those at the top of hierarchical structures. There is a fundamental problem with this. Is this leadership?

The traditional perspective

If we say that leadership is a position in a hierarchy then only a handful of people will ever experience it and most of those will be men. The explanation here will show that leadership is not about position. In fact this perception in society is shaping how leadership is often seen by many as something manipulative, involving power over people, often corrupt and not something many people want to associate with. Hence individuals will comment: 'I'm not a leader, nor do I want to be'. This rejection is based on a wide misconception about leadership which is affecting our world in a very negative way. As Michael Simmons says,

'The history of traditional leadership sits like a heavy weight upon the shoulders of most people'.[1]

At the same time, this misconception also forces people everywhere to view leadership as something for only a few 'special' charismatic individuals. This has created a tendency for most people to sit back and wait for a 'hero' or 'heroine' to put things right in the world. The outcome is a society where people avoid responsibility, put blame on others, encourage those who influence the world to be unaccountable and allow those who exert force to dominate.

Now, with a decade of fast change people are again looking for 'leaders' to fix things, and a perceived crisis in leadership on a global scale has emerged. Articles abound with titles such as 'What's happened to leadership?'[2] and 'Why don't we produce great leaders today?'.[3] As we have seen, research worldwide has identified leadership as an issue for organizations. Yet the present training programmes and academic courses are not resolving the issue. What has happened? Is the answer to find a 'special' leader to solve all our problems? Or does the answer lie elsewhere?

A different story

In 1999, as they had done 20 years previously, people queued to see a film about a group of people who develop their capabilities and use them to fight the terror and evil that is threatening them. It begins:

A long time ago, in a galaxy far, far away . . .

Listening to some of those people in the queues in 1999, it was clear they were looking to connect to something they felt within themselves. In our hearts we know, like the two managers at the financial company who spoke to me about the missing part of themselves not yet identified and expressed in the world, that the human race has the ability to prevail in the face of danger, which is shown in the story of the *Star Wars* films.

There is a part of the human spirit that has yet to be expressed much more widely in the world.

Today, there is a need to search for leadership throughout society so that we can evolve to the next stage of our human existence. John Gardner wrote: 'The reservoir of unused human talent and energy is vast . . . Among the untapped capabilities are leadership gifts'.[4]

Every now and then a situation occurs to an individual and this gift rises to the surface. Yet most people never realize they have this gift: it is this realization that needs to change to enable people to develop the world they desperately want. Robert Greenleaf asked who the enemy is: 'Who is holding back more rapid movement to the better society that is reasonable and possible with available resources? Who is responsible for the mediocre performance of so many of our institutions? Who is standing in the way of a larger consensus on the definition of the better society and paths to reaching it? Not evil people. Not stupid people. Not apathetic people. Not the "system". Not the protesters, the disrupters, the revolutionaries, the reactionaries. . . . The real enemy is fuzzy thinking on the part of good, intelligent, vital people, and their failure to lead'.[5]

In 1982, Tom Peters and Robert Waterman published *In Search of Excellence*, which showed that 'excellence' in organizations was not only possible but was in fact very often in front of our own eyes – but we do not always see it. There was a belief at the time that excellence was only present in Japanese companies.

Now, almost two decades on, *In Search of Leaders* will show that there is not a shortage of leaders, as is presently believed – we just cannot see them in front of us. Reading this book will be such a challenge in perception. Some of what you will read and learn in this book will be difficult to agree with at first because it challenges our present-day thinking and we are comfortable with that. For others, it will stretch your imagination and put your own thoughts into context. This is the first of two books on leadership. Here we focus on you, the individual, and people everywhere. The second book will show what organizations need to do to enable people to practise their leadership. Both are needed.

The premise of *In Search of Leaders* is that the only crisis in leadership is one of perception and understanding. As long as we perceive leadership as mysterious and rare, it will be. As long as we sit back and wait for a hero or heroine to come along and put the world right we will wait forever. In this book the task will be to show that leadership is no more mysterious than being human. For a brief moment, I would like to take you to the case study from my first book, where I found examples of leadership that were truly human and not based on hierarchy as team members were often the same rank.

It begins with the stories of two individuals doing the same job, for the same organization. The job is team leader of the Red Arrows; the organization is the Royal Air Force. They both talk about how they found leadership. How much of their stories can you relate to?

The journey in search of leaders starts here.

Steve's story

I joined the RAF straight from school where I had already experienced practising leadership. I enjoyed many sports and became captain of some, including rugby. I'm not a natural academic learner but through hard work I achieved the academic results eventually. I was Head Boy and a senior rank in the Air Training Corps while at school. In school, just as today, I'm a grafter and put 200% in what I do and it usually pays off. I've never read a book on leadership but for me, leadership is when a group of individuals move forward together in harmony to achieve what you want to achieve and be happy to do it.

When I joined the RAF I had an immature desire to fly and was given responsibility at an early stage. But is that leadership? I found people either stagnate or blossom and the organization gives more to those who appear to be able to take it. It enabled me to practise using assets to achieve things which included people. Even on a squadron you need to handle this leadership well. We tend to teach our pilots to lead in this way from day one. They give briefings two or three times a day; practise presentational skills and instructional skills. So we are equipped with different tools.

However, the RAF as an organization doesn't grow leaders as fast as it could. There's no formal teaching of management and leadership apart from the leadership training I had at 18. It's learning by example, learning from your peers, subordinates and senior officers. So you learn from your mistakes.

In the bigger picture I feel we could introduce ongoing training on leadership and management. We don't teach people to manage. There are two or three structured points in your career at which you can take advanced staff training but it's not used well enough. It tends to concentrate on defence studies and too much reading and writing. It could be better used by, for example, bringing in an outside person to explain new management concepts and ideas on leadership.

Being part of the Reds and then team leader has given me many learning points. In my second year as a team member I became one of the synchro pilots, which was like hanging on with your fingernails to learn as there isn't a lot of time to get it right. The following year I was synchro leader so had to teach the new second-year pilot. There are no manuals but I had plenty of guidance from the boss (Red 1) and others around me. I constructed my own way of teaching by breaking up the manoeuvres, analysing them and then putting them together into a package. There are rules of dos and don'ts and you put these across.

However, the biggest thing I learned while on the team was tolerance both in flying and of individuals' personal faults. As a bolshy bachelor, tolerance hadn't been in my vocabulary. No team is perfect because people rub each other up the wrong way. But a team that can build tolerance is the most successful and in the Reds you learn that everyone can make a mistake but that you learn from it and move on rather than blame. A couple of years later I returned as team leader after learning about leadership running the Harriers out in Germany.

You may think that because the Reds are established the role of team leader will be easy and think everything runs on rails and so you don't have to do very much – but that is a totally wrong view. For me the challenges were having to sort out temporary accommodation at RAF Cranwell, reduction in manpower, the long life of the aircraft and equipment, and lots of other management issues causing problems. They've also all come at once so it's been very busy and learning on the hoof. But I was ready for the experience.

The team had been doing a great deal of touring around the world and while they were away the squadron had been restructured with reductions in manpower. The engineers who maintain the planes had very low morale and were left to themselves to deal with the changes. There had been no consolidation because many had been abroad. I had to pick up the pieces and make the structure work or restructure it again. I worked with individuals on moving forward together.

It was hard because the systems that had been set in stone when we were at RAF Scampton were no longer applicable. People's responsibilities and duties were changed so I delegated to a far greater degree. There was no time to look over their shoulders and check everything except to make sure the quality standards and safety were maintained. Engineering didn't like the change so I remained positive and kept 'selling' it to the workforce. The courage test was when I allowed them to get it wrong and learn. So we had a period of lots of mistakes – but through the learning we achieved the desired results.

Am I a leader? If it means that you are concerned for people and delegate so that we all work in the right direction, the answer is 'yes'. I can now see the difference between management and leadership. Leadership has now become something I do everyday but don't think about. The lesson has been that you are always learning – even from the people underneath you. *If you stop learning – there's something wrong.*

Andy's story

I had no idea I had leadership capabilities and school certainly didn't bring any out. I never took part in any team events or anything. I lived a long way from school so had to catch a bus, walk and catch a train twice every day and always felt alone as my friends in the village all went to the Secondary Modern and I went to the Grammar School. I couldn't leave fast enough and had only a couple of O levels. On leaving school I became an apprentice mechanic and completed this. However, I realized from the outset that I was 'different'. I was full of ideas of how to do things better, faster, and found I could influence people, including the foreman, and events around me.

I joined the RAF not to lead people, but because I was dissatisfied with the job I was doing and knew I could do better. I also needed to get out of the small village where I lived and knew that whatever I achieved in life, it was not going to be where I was. I went into the careers office for the RAF to join as a mechanic but needed another O level. Among the information I found a brochure on flying which told me I needed a minimum of five O levels – so I'd need another three. They looked very sceptical at me as I said I'd like to try to become a pilot. But I managed to convince the RAF to take me as a pilot with four O levels as I was now obsessive about it. Only about 1% of pilots get in with just O levels. They thought I'd never do it – but I did. So began home study over nine months, which cost a fortune and all my earnings went on getting the two additional O levels. A week's wages alone went on one exam. But it was worth it when I passed.

I sailed through Officer Training and joined my first squadron in Germany. I still didn't see myself as a leader at this time. On my next tour I became a flying instructor and experienced leadership for the first time. I felt I was capable of promotion, though I did not have a burning ambition. When I joined the Reds Arrows it was a dream come true and during this time I observed a leader who became the biggest single influence on my own leadership.

He was very different to most of the other leaders I had observed at close quarters. Everyone respected him; he was always calm, thoughtful, purposeful and delegated well. He made everything look easy and everyone was happy and worked hard. Of the other leaders, one in particular chose to take on too many responsibilities personally and many lacked honesty. Many of these leaders retained their position of authority because the 'system' demanded and expected it and because they were usually competent aviators – but few had the respect of their subordinates.

During my last year as a team member of the Red Arrows there was a series of accidents which had a big effect on me. There were three in total, including a fatality, which affected all of us. The final accident was a result of a pilot showing off in front of a camera. He survived but from it I learned the most important lesson: to ensure the right people joined the team.

During my hand-over period as the new leader, it was apparent that one of the existing team members had not reached the required standard after a year on the team. I observed him, flew with him and even had to talk him through a relatively straight-forward emergency when he froze. My mind was made up and discussions with the other team members strengthened my belief even more. He had to go. I set off to tell my boss of my bombshell decision, absolutely determined to get my way. I decided I would turn down the job as leader if I did not. Reluctantly, he accepted my decision. I also tightened the selection process for new team members – including a tough new flying test. I did not want to see anybody else get hurt – physically or otherwise.

As team leader I increased delegation, which had been dismantled in between, and everyone seemed to love it because it gave people more interest and they felt more of a team. As my skills developed, I realized my role wasn't just about flying an aeroplane I also learned that you had to be strong and I never ducked an issue. In fact I always prepared my case carefully if I was proposing something new. I would not let go until I achieved whatever it was I had to fight for. I felt strength from the team – batting on their behalf.

I also found the ability to stand back and be totally objective, which may have seemed aloof but it helped me. A team leader can't be one of the 'boys' and I've always been a bit of a loner. I don't need people patting me on the back and so on. I wanted there to be a close-knit team but I also wanted there to be no doubt where the buck stopped.

It's also important to know when to leave. When you put so much into a job, there's a time to leave before you get stale. I felt three years was enough. Look at Marks & Spencer, where the same people go up and up and up instead of bringing in new thinking to challenge things.

Officer training for leadership didn't really help. The first four months in the RAF is a bit of a game, jumping through hoops. You weren't allowed to bring out your own personality. It was a case of 'this is our model of a leader' then they watch you to ensure you demonstrate exactly this model. I don't think it was real leadership training. If you weren't how they thought you should be, points were taken off. So you play the game with trainers, who are considered by some in the organization to be 'losers' and not leaders themselves as training is considered a sideways move.

What helped me was learning about myself, learning from others, and preparing myself for two years before returning to the Reds as leader. During that time I watched others around me, how they behaved, and then thought through how I would do things. So when I became team leader I knew what was right.

1

The Story of Leadership

Passion generates energy and the capacity for hard work. Just as well, determination and tenacity are all needed.

Charles Handy

What can we learn about leadership from the two stories of the Red Arrows team leaders? The first observation is that they are no different from many other stories I have heard over the years. Apart from flying fast jets, how much could you relate to?

Flying was Steve's passion and he was extremely good at it. I first met him in 1992 when he was leading the synchro pair in the team. What comes out of his story is how each experience enabled him to learn about himself and others around him. When he took on the role of team leader of the Red Arrows he had to look deep inside himself and use his unique capabilities to deal with all the issues the job threw at him and still produce a world-class result from the team. Steve always had this ability in him but he had to find it himself.

When the Red Arrows moved to their temporary accommodation at RAF Cranwell, it was such a disappointment after RAF Scampton, which always felt like home. But they have made Cranwell a 'temporary home' by filling up the walls with photographs and memories. The aeroplanes are over 20 years old and need careful looking after, yet with this equipment they are the best aerobatics team in the world.

Like Steve, Andy had been a superb pilot. Through his learning and searching within himself, Andy applied his leadership gifts and became one of the best team leaders the Red Arrows have known.

Being team leader of the Red Arrows gave both these individuals the ability to use their leadership gifts as never before. Unfortunately, across the armed services, there is a tendency for people to become managers rather than leaders because this is what gets rewarded in a hierarchy. This lack of leadership arises in most corporates today for the same reason.

Many of the issues and frustrations experienced by the military are shared in many other areas. In the same way as corporations and public sector organizations are facing change, the armed forces are facing enormous transformation. Warfare used to have a clear set of rules, a clear understanding of the threat being faced. Now there are new vulnerabilities, which mean the men and women in the armed forces have to think differently. This means people have to break out of their mental models and spend less time thinking about what worked in the past. Today, they have to ask: 'What's possible in the future?'. They have to work through scenarios that are bold and different. This same challenge is facing all organizations.

Did you find that you could relate to or even empathize with parts of the two personal stories? Read the two stories again, only this time take a highlighter pen and use it every time you come to a part where you have had a similar experience.

Everyone has a unique story

These two stories of discovering leadership are quite different. For one it was school sports which enabled leadership gifts to develop, while in the second story being a leader was not even considered until later in life. Becoming a leader is an individual process and fundamental to the process is 'learning'. However, the learning is not through 'training' alone, but through personal experience and learning from that experience. When learning from experience occurs, it involves looking inwards at who we are. It means a deep awareness of who we are and the sort of human being we want to become. Once we know this, it can be expressed in our relationships and actions at work.

Leadership is a personal gift and unique in every human being. Every individual has some gift of leadership. The problem is, most do not know it and many never realize it. In organizations today, the perception of leadership is based on what individuals do rather than as an expression of who they are. For this reason, most books on leadership are studies of chief executives which look for similarities and common traits. The reality is that you could take any group of people and find common threads of leadership – these are not necessarily restricted to designated company heads.

In addition, these common threads are then 'taught' on courses with the underlying belief that if these are what leaders do, others can also be leaders by doing the same things. People cannot be moulded to be the same. Individuals will express leadership in their own way. Andy and Steve used role models for guidance and learning, but each expressed his leadership in his own unique way.

Andy also went through a personal journey inwards while a member of the Red Arrowss following accidents and the death of a team member. He promised himself that when he became team leader he would ensure that there would be no accidents. So one of the changes he brought in was a flying test to ensure a minimum standard of capability for pilots. This test is still part of the process of becoming a Red Arrow. He also always spent five minutes alone before a display to focus his thoughts.

In other words, Andy expressed his leadership in his own unique way – as has every team leader, some better than others. Both Andy and Steve have been good leaders. Both have experienced an inward journey following events in their private and professional lives and both recognize that the day they stop learning, they stop being a leader. Finally, both recognize that each is different, with their own unique strengths and weaknesses. For leadership is an expression of being human.

The experiences of Steve and Andy took them on a difficult journey of learning and discovery: a journey in search of their leadership. It is a journey every human being is capable of. Leadership is part of being human and as such some gift of leadership is in everyone.

But today at large, leadership is perceived as a position for singling out individuals to 'take charge'. This has encouraged other people to behave helplessly and without responsibility. This behaviour begins at school and continues throughout working life, creating a reality akin to the following story by Anthony De Mello:[1]

A man found an eagle's egg and put it in a nest of a barnyard hen. The eagle hatched with the brood of chicks and grew up with them.

All his life the eagle did what the barnyard chicks did, thinking he was a barnyard chicken. He scratched the earth for worms and insects. He clucked and crackled. And he would thrash his wings and fly a few feet into the air.

Years passed and the eagle grew very old. One day he saw a magnificent bird above him in the cloudless sky. It glided in graceful majesty among the powerful wind currents, with scarcely a beat of its strong golden wings.

The eagle looked up in awe. 'Who's that?' he asked.

'That's the eagle, the king of the birds,' said his neighbour. 'He belongs to the sky. We belong to the earth – we're chickens.' So the eagle lived and died a chicken, for that's what he thought he was.

Inside do you feel there are heights to which you could soar? Do you know others who also feel they have much more to offer the world but don't know how? We can see this story reflected in people everywhere and we need to face this head on and accept what is happening in many organizations.

Keeping eagles on the ground

Today in the UK, we still see millions of people heading for work every day either using inadequate public transport or jamming the roads with cars. Not a week goes by without a new story on strife in the workplace – whether long hours, stress, harassment or low morale. In *Working Ourselves to Death*, Diane Fassel wrote: 'Everywhere I go it seems people are killing themselves with work, busyness, rushing, caring and rescuing',[2] while an article in *Fortune* on stamina said: 'Brains are useful. But these days it could be your stamina that really counts. Downsizing forces survivors to work ever long hours, and the global economy has stretched the executive itinerary to China, Indonesia and Malaysia. Mind and body end up in faraway places trying to adjust to new times, new climates, and new germs'.[3]

Why is working life causing so much anxiety for many people? Is the solution to balance our lives better or is it something else?

Organizational structure

For many, the present organizational structure is a problem. We have to stop perceiving organizations as structures of boxes and boundaries. American poet A. R. Ammons wrote:[4]

> Don't establish the
> boundaries
> first
> the squares, triangles,
> boxes
> of preconceived
> possibility,
> and then
> pour
> life into them, trimming
> off left-over edges,
> ending potential:
>
> let centres
> proliferate
> from
> self-justifying motions!

Organizations are living systems of human beings who, if confined, will become drones with suppressed spirits. In this situation, they will be unable to know or express their leadership. Let's ditch the labels of human 'resources', 'headcount' and 'manpower' and create structures that enhance the different talents and capabilities of unique human beings. Among smaller, new organizations is a growing number that are achieving this – but not enough. A radical approach is needed to get structures right for people to use their leadership potential.

Culture

Culture in organizations can be difficult to change. Culture is like fog – you know its there but it's difficult to touch. Culture is deep, entrenched and powerful in its impact on how groups of people work together and how individuals achieve their daily tasks. Culture determines what behaviour is acceptable in an organization, and it is in these norms and beliefs where resistance to change most forcefully resides.

Culture can be on three levels: the routines, habits and repetitive procedures that people are so used to they are sometimes unaware of even doing them; the second level consists of the rules, controls, budgets, measurement systems and training programmes which people are aware of as they affect them on a day-to-day level; the third part of culture deals with the more conceptual areas such as creativity, risk, vision, research, initiatives and transformation. Most change programmes only deal with a part of the culture and result in little, if any, change.

Values

For many individuals in organizations, the issue concerning them is one of values – again, deep, entrenched and powerful in their impact on how individuals work together and achieve their daily tasks. These values determine what behaviour is acceptable and it is in these long-held values where resistance to change at the individual level most forcefully resides. Companies have tried to change this by writing a set of values, which they then inform everyone is now part of the organization. Of course, this often makes little impact because there is no ownership of those values by people – even if they agree with them – because they were not involved in the process of developing them.

Change

Trying to change these three areas are individuals working in human resource departments. Author Alan Briskin tells a wonderful story of three HR people who are asking themselves the question – were we naive?[5] The discussion evolves around their beliefs, which they agree are personal development, collective problem solving, empowerment, self-managing groups, partnerships, customer focus, learning and so on. The three discuss their values, which are honesty, trust and feedback. They then ask how deeply held beliefs within organizations such as commitment to value people, to be tolerant of mistakes and support fairness make them unprepared for the haphazard way people are actually treated, the way mistakes are not forgiven and the ambiguity of fairness. The discussion they have among themselves goes like this:

> I don't think values are enough, or maybe they get in the way – in the way of reality – the reality that we're in business, that we really don't give a shit about people, that we tell people change is good, when it's a mixed blessing.[6]

There must be a thousand people working in HR feeling the same today – and a thousand who haven't reached this point yet. Added to which they are being told 'we need leaders, do something to develop this'.

My experience has found that change is not necessarily more difficult in those who have been in the organization the longest – what is important is *where* they are in the organization. A manager will find change more difficult than an employee; a senior manager will have more difficulty than a project manager; a director will have more difficulty than a functional head. This seems to be because as people worked themselves up the hierarchy, they were being rewarded for their behaviour. So reward and behaviour are linked. This is probably why managers and directors say one thing and do another, causing greater scepticism in the workplace. What remains is hierarchical thinking, which states 'I'm the boss, so I know best', leading to the untapped potential of much of the workforce, particularly in their leadership potential.

Rhetoric and practice

This is not just a UK phenomenon. A survey by the European Foundation for the Improvement of Living and Working Conditions[7] shows 10 EU countries behaving likewise. Using data from nearly 6000 managers from manufacturing, service and the public sector, it found only 2% of those organizations questioned were based on well-trained and qualified employees working in groups with high levels of trust. However, the report also points out that fundamental to this was the large gap between management rhetoric and practice.

In other words, behaviour is inconsistent with the language spoken and so nothing really changes, thus leading to scepticism, mistrust, not knowing what is going on and heavier workloads. The consequences of this cocktail are now showing in the form of greater stress for people at work. For some time there has been significant scientific evidence of a link between our psychological and physical well-being. Feeling that we have some influence over our lives helps to keep us healthy, psychologically and physically. Feelings of lack of control, insecurity, fear of failure and low self-esteem can affect our immune and cardiovascular systems. We know that downsizing has been a culprit of this but it is not the only factor by far.

Stress

For a decade we have been reading articles on how stress is costing organizations in both the private and public sectors. Yet organizations have still not recognized a more pervasive player in the area of stress at work: management. Stress today is not the personal problem of an individual; it is an organizational problem. People cannot operate to their potential, including using their leadership gifts, when under stress.

In one of the widest studies into stress in the workplace, researchers at Warwick University[8] included 16 European countries and analysed 7500 workers. The study showed that British workers were among the most stressed in Europe along with employees in the former East Germany, Greece and Italy. The poignant finding was a growing feeling of alienation as one in five workers said they experienced feeling a 'worthless person' at work and up to one third said they had lost confidence in themselves. In work stress affects performance, affects our motivation levels, the energy we can commit to an action, whether we can use our leadership gifts, and the way we interact with colleagues and customers, as well as the ability to solve problems and make decisions.

Long hours

In the private sector another factor – long hours – is causing stress. The long-hours culture and its knock-on effects on our lives afflict every social class and most types of worker, from long-distance lorry drivers to advertising executives running multi-million pound accounts. A long-hours culture is difficult to change and leads to 'games' such as people leaving a jacket on the chair or a briefcase open when they go home so that others will think they are still in the building. How did this start? People were rewarded for the long hours they put in with promotion and others were expected to behave likewise and copied this behaviour. A report[9] shows that the problem of people working long hours is worse in the USA than in any other industrialized country, beating Japan, Korea, Hong Kong and Singapore where hard work is part of the culture.

As long ago as the 1960s researchers in California[10] found that for people aged under 45, deaths from heart disease doubled if they worked 48 hours a week, compared with those working fewer than 40 hours. In the UK, the average employee works 43.1 hours a week, and a quarter of the workforce spend more than 60 hours a week at work, according to *Parents at Work*.[11] The law has changed to reduce working hours but loopholes have maintained working hours far higher than in the rest of Europe. Long hours are now perceived as a factor involved in train drivers in the UK going through red lights and causing accidents.

Someone who has researched into long hours is Professor Cary Cooper, who says 'It's not long hours that count, it's working well. Britain has developed a culture like the USA where work comes first and family second'.[12]

In 1998 *Management Today* and *WFD* surveyed nearly 6000 managers and found that 53% of men and 48% of women worked between 41 and 50 hours per week. Another 28% of men and 18% of women worked more than 51 hours a week. However, while more than 78% of managers worked more than 40 hours, the figures were down on the previous year. Today more and more men and women are saying they would rather not have the promotion or pay rise if instead they could have more time with their families and loved ones.

While many feel compelled to work long hours, they concede that it adversely affects their health, their morale, their productivity and their relationships with partners and children. A total of 72% said the long-hours culture affected their relationship with their partners and 73% said it had an effect on relationships with their children. So the values of individuals are changing but those at the top of organizations who were rewarded for long hours encourage the culture to remain the same.

Working long hours was seen as entirely acceptable by 45% of senior managers and directors. Over a third of middle and junior managers, on the other hand, only work long hours because they think they have to, and 22% said they found it unacceptable, but had no choice.

Job satisfaction

The *Management Today* report also found that the difference between directors and managers is apparent in other areas, including job satisfaction. Chairmen, chief executives and managing directors record relatively high levels of satisfaction with their job security, downward communication, career opportunities, recognition for performance and feedback. However, at senior manager level, only 18% feel secure in their jobs; the figure falls to 11% for middle managers and to just 9% for junior managers. When it comes to communication, 19% of senior managers are satisfied, compared to 6% of middle managers. Alarmingly, junior managers scored −8% in satisfaction with communication, which suggests a feeling of not knowing what is going on and being permanently in the dark.

When it came to recognition, only 4% of middle managers felt they received recognition for their performance and 8% said they were happy with their pay. On the subject of career opportunities less than 5% of middle managers were satisfied; this percentage is declining every year.

In regard to present restructuring, a slight majority think it has helped profitability, but more think it has harmed morale and loyalty, and caused the loss of essential skills and experience. Finally, in the report, managers were asked to give advice to directors on what is lacking in their work. The top two were 'greater consultation and involvement' and 'greater investment in and rewards for people'. Above all, they want deeds not words – which is exactly what they are not getting.

How does this affect leadership? Feeling out of control, and having low morale and poor job satisfaction suppress any leadership talent, while taking initiative or risks is frowned upon by managers.

Cost of success

Following up this study, in 1999 *Management Today* published *Price of Success*,[14] which showed that almost half the British workforce feel so undervalued and stressed in their jobs, that they want to leave. Of the 1666 managers interviewed, 37% said they would leave their jobs within the next year because of lack of recognition for what they did, 35% because they felt that their jobs gave them a poor quality of life, and 22% because of stress. Even more alarming, the study found that one quarter of women and one fifth of men had turned to alcohol to ease the pressure.

This is clear evidence that when leadership is perceived to be at the top of a hierarchy, even a flatter hierarchy, the rest of the organization feels powerless and abused. Leadership cannot be expressed by the majority of people in these organizations and training is not the solution on its own.

Positive actions

Some organizations are taking positive action. Price Waterhouse (now Price Waterhouse Coopers) was motivated to change when management realized that the company was losing too many good people, particularly women. However, their response was not to target women for special treatment but rather to give responsibility to individuals through a flexible choice system called the Flex System. This gives the workforce a menu of options, ranging from membership of leisure clubs and extra holidays to childcare vouchers or health and accident insurance. Individuals 'buy' from the menu according to their needs and desires. There are now signs that loyalty has improved and women are staying on because they can resolve their childcare issue. Although childcare has been considered a women's issue, it is really a family issue and a human issue.

The UK offices of a well-known global food company had the same problem of losing good women. However, their solution was to train women to be more assertive so they could be more like the men. The culture is very 'macho' and management gets rewarded for this behaviour. An executive said: 'We have lots of good training, but its aim is to strip you of your individuality and then build you into the corporate mould'.

The key difference between the two companies is that the first took into account the motivations and feelings of its people. Kevin Thomson argues: 'Harnessing and managing knowledge is one thing, but organizations need to manage emotions, feelings and beliefs that motivate people to apply that knowledge constructively. Then, and only then, can a company's lifeblood – emotional capital – make an impact on financial performance'.[15] When this happens, people can use all their potential, including their leadership, which will positively benefit staff, customers and financial targets.

The worst case

The worst reports of recent times are on individuals who abuse people at work. The TUC has completed some research[16] into bullying and has found examples ranging from off-the-cuff shouting and swearing, to calculated humiliation. One manager forced employees to stand in the corner of the room wearing a dunce's cap if he thought they were not working hard enough. At first it may seem silly, but see yourself as one of those people and feel what it feels like. It's not so silly now, is it?

The analysis from the TUC report suggests that many of the middle managers responsible for intimidation had suffered similar treatment when they were younger. There seems to be a view that some managers who were on the first rung of the corporate ladder during the cut and thrust of the Thatcher era are now causing problems in positions of power. When leadership is based on power and position there will be those who take advantage of having power over others. People only stay until they can find another job, which is not easy, and the longer this situation goes on, the harder it is for an individual to cope. The ironic thing is that bullies suffer from low self-esteem which is never resolved.

An example is a managing director of a company from the mobile phone industry. He was often known to 'blow up' and have tantrums. He issued threats to managers, who were told that they had to attend monthly managers' meetings – even though they were after hours, with no refreshments, and travel costs were never covered. He even used this approach to invite staff to the annual ball, and lack of attendance at either of these often resulted in sackings.

Every day he would shout and swear at area managers about sales figures. One of these area managers would in turn shout and swear at branch managers every hour of every day. It was the area manager's experience of being managed and now he was copying. Not surprisingly, staff turnover was high and the company was taken to court for unfair dismissal more than once. However, this company was making money and so respect for people – whether staff or customers – was not important. Today, with greater competition, the director is trying to sell his company and make a quick killing before driving off in his Ferrari. The area manager has since left.

Future work

What about work in the future? Will leadership have the opportunity to be expressed by a larger educated workforce? In a report entitled *Tomorrow's People*, by the London Human Resource Group,[17] the important finding was that 'new ways of thinking are more important than new ways of working in achieving the necessary flexibility in today's workplace'. It claims that by concentrating on new forms of working, public discussion of the flexible labour market has ignored an important requirement that has already developed and will continue to do so in the future – 'mindset flexibility'.

The report argues that the new mindset has to deal with 'three harsh facts'. The first is that instead of the security of a job for life, security is now based on performance rather than paternalism. Secondly, people at work have to treat their employers as customers of their labour services. This means employees see themselves as self-employed, keen to retain their customer's business, be rewarded in accordance and acquire progressive skills that improve their employability inside and outside their current organization. Finally, employees need to realize that although their employers will provide training that helps with the acquisition of progressive skills, substantive responsibility for development will rest with themselves. This moves the individual from being subservient, with no control, to an influencing, committed worker.

This approach has been called the new employment deal. However, in many places this whole concept has failed to materialize, according to Professor Amin Rajam. He is the principal author of a report commissioned by the CBI, TUC, Cabinet Office and leading companies.[18]

It states: 'The skills and attributes that individuals need to cope with the emotional insecurity associated with the concept of employability are not there in many organizations. . . . Part of the trouble is that, as with every other area of people management, managers have completely misunderstood the scope of what they are attempting to do, overestimated their capacity to do it, and underestimated the cynicism their behaviour would cause'.

In particular, the report shows that 95% of companies lack the leadership at all levels to motivate people in a climate of rapid change. It concludes that the skills, sensitivity and expertise in human resource departments to resolve this remain to be developed in many organizations.

As Abraham Maslow said: 'For centuries human nature has been sold short'.[19] Therefore, leadership is again suppressed by what I call the 'management mindset' – how managers think and see the world.

Succession planning

Another concern for developing leaders in organizations is succession planning. There seems to be a stalemate between the old hierarchical organization and the new flatter one. Real challenges should be made available in the workplace and these should be rewarded with recognition, which does not only mean promotion. At the same time, high flyers have to change their mindset, which is still stuck at being motivated by reaching 'the top'. Power and jostling for position is the old way but again continues because those in senior positions were rewarded in this way and continue to dish out the same reward. This is just one illustration to show that organizations are still hierarchical and, more important, so is the thinking. Leadership is still perceived as position.

A new consciousness

Today, people are asking why they should sell their souls to companies willing to downsize at a moment's notice. Why should they work ever more punishing hours to earn more money if they are then too exhausted to enjoy the extra income? People are rethinking their priorities and redefining the notions of success and fulfilment. The dictionary defines success as attainment of wealth, fame or position. There is strong evidence of the UK becoming like the USA, where selfish capitalism is rife with a race of 'wannabe' and 'wannahave' individuals, and there is evidence that those influenced by Thatcherism have taken that route. However, there is a definite movement towards another view of success seen on both sides of the Atlantic as stipulated by the great American inventor, Emerson:[20]

> To laugh often and much; to win the respect of intelligent people and the affection of children; to earn the appreciation of honest critics and to endure the betrayal of false friends; to appreciate beauty; to find the best in others; to leave the world a bit better whether by a healthy child, a garden patch, or a redeemed social condition; to know that even one life has breathed easier because you lived; this is to have success.

Generation X

The workforce in many parts is changing and with it, an attitude to work which is yet to reach board level. Driving this change have been women wanting flexibility but today broader change is also being driven by the new aspirations of 'Generation X'. A study from the Leadership Institute of Southern California[21] compared Generation X, born between 1965 and 1981, and their predecessors, the Baby Boomers (1943–1964). The research found four X traits which have implications for today's workplace and leadership in the future:

- The need for balance between work and private life stemming from being the children of parents who both worked. It was found they felt deprived of their parents' company, reinforced by the fact that a very high percentage were children of divorced parents. Therefore, this group want more time for family life.

- The need for mobility. They believe that better challenges and salaries come from changing companies rather than waiting to move up a ladder in one. They see each job as building skills for the next and view loyalty as being due to oneself and colleagues, not to a boss or company.
- Total fluency with computers, which they have grown up with. Older generations need to harness this knowledge, not restrain it.
- A strong need for a workplace which feels like a community. This is their preferred workplace environment and teamwork is central to it.

This environment is difficult in a hierarchy with managers jostling for position. A new type of organization is required which will allow teams and communities to flourish and leadership to be expressed throughout.

Charles Handy, in his book *Beyond Certainty*, says that Generation X men and women are questioning whether working life as it is at present is worth it. He adds: 'The idea that organizations can own people's time and brains is looking increasingly out of date'. Handy suggests 'organizations will have to become communities rather than properties; with members, not employees'.[22]

Birbeck College studied 600 graduates[23] and found that even before they start work, the graduates are determined not to sacrifice their lives for their careers and do not believe that long hours will result in promotion. However, the graduates are very committed to the organizations they work for. When asked what aspects of a career were particularly important, 87% rated work they enjoyed and 64% said an intellectually challenging job. This compared to 15% rating rapid promotion and only 11% a large salary. The challenge is going to be whether organizations will meet these changing desires or whether these young people will end up complying.

What bosses want

If we change this around and instead establish the needs of those in so-called 'leadership' positions, we can see that they are still stuck in an old paradigm of thinking which sees workers without brains. A study by Andersen Consulting[24] found that employers are looking for young people who are 'job ready' – capable of fitting into their organizations quickly and easily and not challenging how things are done. In other words, those at the top want compliance, not leadership, in their organizations.

Enthusiasm and a willingness to work hard doing what they were told were more important than qualifications, according to the report. In fact, only 9% of the one hundred leading employers mentioned qualifications at all. It seems learning and thinking are not required even though they talk of 'knowledge workers'. More than a third mentioned communication and interpersonal skills. Nearly half of those surveyed said it was difficult to find young people who were keen, flexible and had the 'right attitude'. They said that schools were not producing the right employees and putting too much emphasis on qualifications. This means that companies that recruit graduates are often anxious about how they will perform and whether the cost of training them is effective.

Surely the issue here is not about what schools and universities are doing if they are producing more individuals with a good education, but rather how the organizations that employ them need to change so that intelligent workers can thrive. It would seem that many employers are still looking for drones who will work with compliance. If this is the case, there is no way leadership can develop in these organizations. However, there are signs that the young generation will not accept this, and this is worth exploring here as it has implications in our search for leaders.

The young speak

A think tank, called *Thoughts for the Millennium*, has been set up by two 20-year-olds.[25] They sent volunteers to nine cities to distribute questionnaires to a wide range of young people. The average age was 19.7 years and a high proportion were in full-time education, mostly at university. The findings showed a high number of budding entrepreneurs who were very determined to control their own success.

It also showed that within this group was a consensus that inherited wealth, class and a private education are no longer prerequisites for success. What drove them was not material wealth but rather realizing ambitions and achieving self-actualization (a concept developed by Abraham Maslow, which in essence means becoming the best you can and living a purposeful life). This generation do not want a leader based on position to do everything for them, including political leaders.

Many of these 20-year-olds felt a high sense of distrust in the political process and saw politics as redundant in many areas. One of the founders of the think tank was on the youth advisory panel for the No. 10 policy unit and his experience was worrying. 'They were more concerned with gimmicks to attract young people – free sports vouchers and free arts vouchers – than educating people about what politics was there to do'.[26]

Mori and WFD[27] carried out a poll among '30 somethings' and found one in five said they were so concerned about the lack of balance between work and home life, they would accept a cut in pay to have more free time. Also, 92% of under 35s felt that the ability to balance work with personal life was very or fairly important. This balance between work and life ranked higher than the quality of their boss and the opportunity of promotion when they were asked what made them committed to their employer. This change is very different from the yuppies of the 1980s. Whereas people today have inherited a heavy workload, they reject the mindset of material rewards for long hours – particularly 18–35-year-olds. Values and priorities have shifted.

We are on the cusp of a change that should be included along with globalization and information technology. It is that of a need to express the human spirit and human potential for something worth while. It is a need to express one's leadership.

Demos, the independent think tank, has produced a European-wide report[28] titled 'Generation X and the new work ethic'. It shows that the 18–34 age group are much less committed to the notion of a regular job than their elders, and are more concerned with developing a portfolio of interests and useful skills. This is also reflected in a global student survey by Coopers and Lybrand.[29] The respondents' number-one priority was to 'achieve a balanced lifestyle and to have a rewarding life outside work'. In terms of importance, they placed 'personal growth' ahead of 'building a career'.

It would appear that a gap is forming between the generations. The 'old school' work on a 'management mindset' that no longer works, but because of their thinking and self-interests they are hanging on to it. This is because many of those who are 'leaders' based on position are now feeling threatened. They fear losing their power base because their position has become their identity, even though many abuse this power. Organizational issues such as sexual harassment are not about sex, but power, as is bullying. Incompetence is left unaccountable because of rules and procedures which protect managers, such as taking early retirement. Innovation, creativity and initiative are suppressed through control mechanisms. The individual is unable to express his or her leadership and training courses alone will not change this.

A paradigm shift

However, we can also find organizations where the opposite is the reality and others will follow or new ones will be created. Today is an exciting time to be alive. We are going through what is termed a 'paradigm shift'. The concept was first used by philosopher and science historian Thomas Kuhn to describe the concepts, techniques and values used by the scientific community. When a change occurs in the paradigm it is revolutionary and called a paradigm shift.

Today, the term is used more widely to define a framework of thinking or a way of understanding reality. It is like entering a black hole in space and emerging from it not knowing what is going to be on the other side. However, just as you are emerging into the hole, there are flashes of different coloured lights which enable you to see something of what will be when you emerge. Some of those lights we are experiencing now.

Lights guiding our path

The first light is the different world which will emerge from information technology. It is beginning to create an open network but it is causing additional workload pressures to individuals at present because it is trying to exist in the old paradigm and existing organizational structures. We have only touched the surface of technology, which will affect every living person. We have yet to use technology to enable individuals to build relationships and resolve the issues affecting us all.

The second light is globalization and becoming one world. An open market-place is emerging for some and causing a paradox, for while there is unprecedented opportunity for some to tap new markets, traditional markets are shrinking or becoming intensely competitive. In my opinion, the most important aim for globalization is world peace, food for all and education for every child. In other words, we should take the challenge of globalization to create a better world for all, not just an economic market-place for mass consumerism where only the well-off benefit.

Finally, the third light has to do with human beings and in parti-cular their knowledge and self-actualization. The younger workforce no longer accepts being told what to do and not question or think for themselves. They want to determine both their work and private lives which they perceive as equally important. Alvin Toffler wrote: 'It is one of the grand ironies of history that a new kind of autonomous employee is emerging who, in fact, does own the means of production. The new means of production however, are not to be found in the artisan's toolbox, or in the massive machinery of the smokestack age. They are instead, crackling inside the employees cranium – where society will find the single most important source of future wealth and power'.[30]

In those heads are the ideas, desires and creativity to change our organizations so they serve the world – a world where values, aspira-tions and self-actualization are as important as technology and profit; a world which is more open and better than we have at present. There is a hunger for expressing our leadership gifts which is not forthcoming in the world at present.

The search continues

At the start of the new millennium we are on a journey in search of leaders – and it is a journey for every human being. It is a journey which Margaret Wheatley describes as 'nothing less than the search for new sources of order in our world'.[31] It is a journey you will participate in as you read this book and, like many journeys, it will involve facing fears and questioning your beliefs. But also, like any journey, it will include new experiences and understanding with the excitement and wonder that new learning and places bring. The starting place is to begin to question the concept we call 'leadership'.

2

The Seven Essences of Leadership

I consider the essence of all religions is a good heart, a peaceful mind, compassion, forgiveness, respect for other lives, a sense of brotherhood, sisterhood. These are the essential message of the various religions. We use the same material, like gold, but we can change the shape according to our practical needs. So similarly religion has the same essence, but the requirement in our daily life is of new approaches.

Dalai Lama

When most people try to understand leadership, they ask for a definition. This is asking: 'what does leadership mean?'. Leadership expressed by individuals will have a variety of meanings. Therefore, definition is subjective and incomplete. Yet many have tried to define leadership. Let us have a look at some of them.

Defining leadership

To an extent, leadership is like beauty: it's hard to define, but you know it when you see it.[1]

Leadership is not domination, but the art of persuading people to work toward a common goal.[2]

If leadership in different times and circumstances has a common thread, it is to face situations actively rather than passively, to overcome and transform conditions, not simply to react and adapt to them.[3]

Leadership is about going somewhere; it's not about wandering around aimlessly.[4]

No one can understand leadership without recognizing that it is, at one and the same time elusive but momentous, passionate but coldly single minded, a matter for patience but sudden opportunity, and a force to be grasped by ambitious individuals but nurtured by others. It is a capacity that flourishes in circumstances that may be hopeless, to achieve ends that may be triumphant or forlorn. In a sense it matters little which, for it is the great struggle for victory which is the ordinary habit of leadership.[5]

Leadership is all about the release of human possibilities.[6]

Leadership, which is observed primarily as a set of behaviours, is influenced, if not determined, by culture and one's life experience.[7]

All leaders are actual or potential power holders, but not all power holders are leaders.[8]

Leadership is disciplined passion.[9]

. . . old stereotypes condition our thinking about leadership and what we think a leader ought to be.[10]

My theory of effective executive leadership, or visionary leadership, considers not only the leader's personal characteristics, not only the leader's behaviour, and not only the situation; it considers all three.[11]

Having read these, are you now wiser about what leadership is? All contribute to our understanding of leadership – but none is 'big' enough to clarify leadership. What becomes clear is that although much has been written on the topic, there is no single definition of leadership – only a personal one. Therefore, another approach is required.

The essence of leadership

According to the dictionary, the word essence means 'most important feature of something which determines its identity'. In the search for leaders, there is an abundance of material which clearly shows that there appear to be essences of leadership and these need clarification. By looking at the essences of leadership, we may gain a better understanding. Therefore, this chapter outlines these essences and how some individuals have explained them. In fact, there is a wealth of knowledge for discovery.

In doing this, the human phenomenon called leadership can be better understood and reveals some surprises. These seven essences sometimes challenge the present-day perception of leadership but leave us with an exciting path forward to transform the present crisis in leadership in society today.

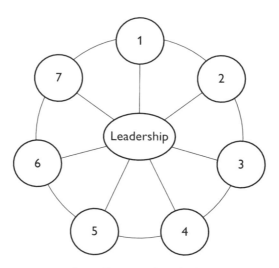

Seven Essences of Leadership

Essence 1

There is a clear distinction between leadership and management.

Tom Peters wrote: 'The difference between managers and leaders is the difference between day and night. The former honour stability, control through systems and procedures. Leaders thrive on change'.[12]

However, more comprehensive and less well known is the work of Professor Abraham Zaleznik of Harvard, who has clearly defined the difference between management and leadership. It began with a paper entitled 'Managers and leaders: are they different?'[13] where he argued that the differences were profound in what each thinks, how they interact, how they work and how they develop.

Management behaviour

Zaleznik expanded his work with the publication of *The Managerial Mystique*, in which he explained that managers tend to adopt an impersonal, passive attitude towards goals, viewing them as a means of getting the job done. As such, managers attempt to solve problems by continually seeking compromise among people and ideas. Managers, he says, 'view themselves as conservators and regulators of an existing order that they personally identify with and from which they gain rewards'.[14]

It is clear within this perspective that decision making is slow and that change is a challenge not only for the organization, but for managers who, having been rewarded for maintaining the status quo, now worry about whether they will still be rewarded in the future.

Zaleznik adds that managers worry more about people's roles than about the people themselves. As such, they enhance their self-worth by perpetuating existing processes and orders. To maintain controlled, rational organizational structures, managers generate red tape and display little directness and warmth. Managers do not ask for the hearts and minds of people, only their performance. This results in a way of thinking whereby problems are taken up one at a time using calculation and compliance and a great deal of politics.

Today in organizations, managers may use the words of winning hearts but their actions show that it is still performance that counts. For Zaleznik, the outstanding characteristic of the managerial mind is that it is programmatic and greatly resistant to change. This explains why we hear the language of change but not the actions. However, Zaleznik adds that there is an optimism and abiding faith in progress from managers but also a denial, which includes the ability to turn a blind eye to errors of omission that result in the slow death of organizations.

Leadership behaviour

In contrast, leaders, according to Zaleznik, adopt a personal and active attitude towards goals, viewing them as a basic reason for being. Here, leaders work in the opposite spirit from managers, attempting to develop fresh approaches to annoying problems. They worry about ideas and how they will affect people, while relating to people in intuitive and empathetic ways, asking: 'What will these events and decisions mean to everyone?' In this perspective, Zaleznik shows that leaders seek opportunities for change as they wish to profoundly alter human, economic and political relationships.

Whereas career managers are likely to exhibit narcissism, according to Zaleznik, leaders do not depend on titles or work roles for their sense of identity. In fact, Zaleznik argues that leaders promote organizational structures that often appear turbulent and even disorganized but they motivate individuals and often produce results beyond those expected. For Zaleznik, leadership goes beyond managing a process. In fact, he argues that leaders are not bound by a process but *challenge* it to produce creative actions.

Fundamentals

However, the key difference for me involves fundamental assumptions that managers and leaders make about people in organizations, about human nature and what is important. This is apparent in Zalenik's work although he does not actually say this. Managers still see human beings as a resource whereas leaders see themselves and others as what makes an organization succeed.

Finally, Zaleznik asks: 'The question that begs for an answer is whether the managerial point of view is an outcome of the way organizations are or whether it comes from the kinds of people who seek and gain power as managers'.[15] This question is fundamental to the future of organizations and the answer is probably an element of both. Hierarchical structures are very difficult to change and they allow certain behaviour to be rewarded. So how has this happened?

According to Professor John Kotter, also of Harvard, the problem arose a century ago when we began creating thousands of large organizations and started to develop 'managers' to run them. For myself and others, the problem began earlier and has been propagated by the past hundred years.

The birth of management

Management was born out of the womb of the Industrial Revolution when the workforce from the countryside moved to work in the new factories. A few individuals were needed to control an uneducated workforce and ensure production outputs. The manager was born.

> The village blacksmith shop was abandoned, the road-side shoe shop was deserted, the tailor left his bench, and all together these mechanics (workers) turned away from their country homes and wandered their way to the cities wherein the large factories had been erected.

> The gates were unlocked in the morning to allow them to enter, and after their daily task was done the gates were closed after them in the evening.

> Silently and thoughtfully, these men went to their homes. They no longer carried the keys of the workshop, for workshop, tools and key belonged not to them, but to their master.[16]

In the 1890s Frederick Taylor began to shape management, particularly in the USA, by establishing the most efficient ways to turn the human body into a mechanism. Two hundred years earlier Isaac Newton had shown the world to be a machine, a big clock, which could be controlled by men. Now Taylor would do the same with the workplace. Even as a child, Taylor forced his friends to use strict rules in their games.

Taylor conceived the 'first class man' concept, which he defined as 'the ability to control yourself, body and mind; the ability to do things which your common sense tells you [you] ought to do; the ability above all to do things which are disagreeable, which you do not like'.[17] The utilitarian movement was gaining hold, speaking of rationality, control and productivity at the time and the brainwashing of these virtues aimed specifically at the market-place.

Today, there is a still a belief that if reengineered, organizations will run like clockwork. But even more fundamental are the remnants of Taylorism in the form of 'blame cultures' and individuals refusing to take responsibility at work. Taylor often told workers, 'You're not supposed to think; there are other people paid for thinking around here'.[18]

If work is rigidly determined by processes and if we are encouraged to believe that thinking is being done for us, then we lose a sense of discovery and a sense of the human spirit. People's learned response is passivity and when they are told that they are now empowered to think, they will be suspicious and afraid of a painful response if they change because they have been rewarded for doing a job and not asking questions.

What you hear is: 'It's not my fault' and 'The system is at fault'.

'New' management

Many argue that management has changed, particularly since the human relations movement during the past thirty years. But has management changed? According to Zaleznik, human relations specialists used psychology to influence managers to change from task to people centredness and from autocratic to democratic orientation. At first managers could be divided between the two extremes. But then managers found that by using some of the psychological techniques, they could manipulate management control.

Today, managers will not simply be theory X or theory Y; they are neither authoritarian nor egalitarian, hostile nor loving. Managers have become what Richard Sennett, Professor of Humanities at New York University, has called 'authority without love'.[19] The authority is detached, non-emotional and based on the notion of using people to get things done. This is how leadership has been perceived in the armed forces and in many organizations. Only now we have created the 'professional manager'. When you look at organizations today, you do not see leaders as much as these new professional managers. In fact, the professional manager has ascended to the top of the power pyramid – some with their MBAs from business schools.

Maintaining this is a control structure of formal budgeting, financial plans, monthly reports, quarterly reviews, capital expenditure planning and projections influencing what managers do. Zaleznik says: 'the effect is to make authority relations revolve around the management process rather than the content of the work'.[20]

Joseph Badoracco and Richard Ellsworth argue that: 'Managers are as much captives as masters of their companies. The management systems and structures that make up the formal organization are powerful instruments for extending a manager's reach'.[21]

Management as a worldview

Zaleznik argues that management control is more than a set of tools. He sees this as itself a 'worldview', integrated into the thinking of this new professional manager. This worldview comes from Newtonian science where the world is a machine to be controlled. Within this worldview are organizations where the control system gives managers the means to direct the behaviour of people.

Margaret Wheatley has pointed out that we have confused control with order and a mechanistic predictability. She wrote: 'for most of its written history, management has been defined in terms of its control functions. Lenin spoke for many managers when he said: "Freedom is good, but control is better"'.[22] Today, managers are trying to grasp any remnant of control in a world that is changing dramatically.

We are in a situation where human resource people are saying, 'we need leaders as well as managers', thus separating what they see as the process people and the people people. Yet leadership is more than this manipulation and cannot thrive in the present worldview.

We saw in the previous chapter that individual leadership is suppressed in organizations today. The reason is because organizations are built and run for managers. Management, whether 'old' or 'new', is about control. Today, the control functions of management (planning, staffing, monitoring, setting goals) are for a world we are leaving behind. It no longer works so managers are fighting for survival, and their strong self-interest, ego and addiction to power are causing pain as our world transforms.

New management ideas as explained by Alan Briskin are:[23]

what began as a method of control for managers to motivate and channel their workers' productivity became instead a failed psychological contract. The promise of being cared for was a hollow offer of false love. Human relations was perched on a contradiction: advocating for personal development and democratic principles on the one hand, and on the other serving in a subordinate role to the increasingly bureaucratic and mechanized workplace.

Leadership goes beyond encouraging and coaching others to seek solutions. Leaders must be able to be involved in the essential element of the required thinking to enable organizations to go beyond solving problems and into the realms of opportunities. Leadership inspires trust and innovation; instead of 'managing' change, leadership creates change. How can this work alongside a control structure with a power-based hierarchy?

Different worlds

Management and leadership are two very different and distinctive worldviews. So is the answer to change managers into leaders? James Champy wrote:[24]

> Everyone must change. The change will go deeper than technique. It touches not merely what managers do, but who they are. Not just their sense of task, but their sense of themselves. Not just what they know, but how they think. Not just their way of seeing the world, but their way of living in the world.

We are talking of a paradigm shift and part of this will include the structure and purpose of organizations. The present structure for most organizations in the world today is the hierarchy. The reason is the belief that it is the best available way of operating. Many of these organizations are talking of changing their structure to cross-functional teams, a task structure or a flatter organization. However, they remain essentially hierarchical in structure, process and thinking. Zaleznik says that hierarchies work when the organization prospers and people have confidence that the few have the best interests of the many in mind. Following downsizing, job insecurity and the rise of knowledge workers, these conditions are weak.

This leads people to question three things, according to Zaleznik. These are satisfaction, belonging and identity. Hierarchy means inequality and its justification as the best way is no longer convincing. The problem is that most managers at the top of these structures do not know what else to do to survive except more and more cost cutting, which is leading to more and more questioning of satisfaction, belonging and identity. Now when managers say, 'Yes, everyone is working harder and we're asking them to do even more with half the staff and resources, but we really care about our people in this place', it just doesn't add up any more.

Hierarchical structures and management belong to an old paradigm which is dying. Leadership cannot be added on to management as it is in many training programmes because it requires a different worldview. Fundamental will be a shift in the perception of leadership by human beings everywhere, which leads to the second essence.

Summary of Essence 1

1. For Zaleznik, leadership goes beyond managing a process. In fact, he argues that leaders are not bound by a process but *challenge* it to produce creative actions.
2. Managers still see human beings as a resource whereas leaders see themselves and others as what makes an organization succeed.
3. Leadership inspires trust and innovation; instead of 'managing' change, leadership creates change.

Essence 2

There has been a debate about whether leaders are born or made since the time of the ancient Greeks. The answer is: both. For within every human being is some gift of leadership, be it greater in some than others. Leadership is the province of all, not the few.

Whenever I have asked delegates or students to describe leaders, they use examples of politicians, historical heroes and heroines, tyrants or entrepreneurs. Their perception is that leaders are somehow special people who have around them power, riches, superiority, status and so on. This is probably how most people perceive leaders and is a view prevalent in society at large today.

James MacGregor Burns said: 'One of the most universal cravings of our time is a hunger for compelling and creative leadership'.[25] What has not yet been realized is that people do not have to look elsewhere for it – they just need to look inside themselves. Looking outside has created a helpless attitude of waiting for a hero or heroine to come and put everything right. Instead, people have the capability themselves, but do not realize it yet.

Joseph Jaworski knew this when he wrote: 'The conventional view of leadership emphasizes positional power and conspicuous accomplishment. But true leadership is about creating a domain in which we continually learn and become more capable of participating in our unfolding future'.[26] He goes on to say that leadership involves creating a field of knowledge to further our understanding of reality whereby people can take part in shaping the future. The fact that we instead sit back and wait for a leader to emerge is how a handful of powermongers do what they do without repercussions. But this is changing and people are beginning to express their own leadership – though not enough yet. We have seen this in the emergence of pressure groups and consumers' actions.

Sally Helgesen says:

> For most, studies of leadership have proceeded from the unspoken presumption that leaders are leaders by virtue of their position. And so if we want to study leadership we study the CEO. It is demoralizing because the relentless aggrandizement of those at the top leads organizations to fall prey to a heroes and drones syndrome, exulting the value of those in powerful positions while implicitly demeaning the contributions of those who fail to reach the top rank.[27]

Would you put your life and future in the hands of a professional manager? Or would you rather develop your own full potential and live in the confidence that no matter what you do or where you are, you will live and work as a free, purposeful human being? Kouzes and Posner concluded that leadership was not the privilege of a few charismatic men and women. Rather, it was what ordinary people use when they bring about the best from themselves and others. Kouzes and Posner say: 'When we liberate the leader in everyone, extraordinary things happen'.[28]

Everyone can be a leader

Imagine telling everyone you work with, everyone you know, that they are leaders. Not only this, but that you can *show* them that it is true and even help them find that leadership based on integrity and purpose beyond selfish desires. A radical transformation would happen. For most people use only a fraction of their leadership potential and the challenges of the world need their full capabilities.

For some, this knowledge is harder to believe than others, particularly for many women and ethnic minorities whom society has not perceived as leaders. They themselves will see leaders as corrupt power holders. Sara Melendez wrote 'An outsider's view of leadership', where she shows that for many of the black population life does not provide them with the opportunities to practise or develop leadership skills. She also says: 'Often expression of passion in white men is lauded, while similar passion is often seen as emotionalism when it is expressed by women, or confrontation when it is expressed by men of color'.[29]

Therefore, there is a great deal of work to be done to enable individuals to find their own leadership gifts. As Margaret Lulic said: 'When we are boxed and labelled by titles, education, sex, race and beliefs, potential from individuals is wasted'.[30] To break out of these boxes and discover leadership, individuals need to develop self-confidence, which comes from learning about ourselves. We have to overcome barriers of limiting beliefs which prevent our leadership gifts being expressed. We have to realize that leadership is for all, not the few. As Joseph Jaworski said: 'Leadership is all about the release of human possibilities'.[31]

Two sides of being human

So how can human beings develop their full potential, including their leadership gifts? The first step is to realize that every one of us has two sides to their being. This was described in Chinese writings as the yin and yang. They are usually seen as the masculine and feminine. However, every human being has some of each. This means that men have some feminine sides to their nature and women have some masculine sides to them. Some men get alarmed at this when it is stated, but that is because of how we stereotype gender in society. Let us put this in the context of leadership.

One of the well-known writers on leadership was Lao-tzu. He recognized that many leaders were seen as powerful warriors who used their might to win battles. This he referred to as the yang or masculine part of leadership. Whether men or women, we have battles in life which test this strength within us, which is both mental and physical. Lao-tzu went on to say that leadership should be more about maintaining an open, receptive and nourishing behaviour. He said that this was the feminine or yin aspect of leadership. He explained this by saying that the yin is like water while the yang is like rock. Water may yield and seem less strong than rock, yet it will wear away rock, which is too rigid to yield. He maintained that the leader knows that gentleness can melt rigid defences and yielding overcomes resistance.

However, in understanding the yin and yang in ourselves, try not to see this as an either/or. We are all both yin and yang at the same time. Each grows and changes as we live our lives, yet neither evolves without the other and neither can live without the other. I know many stories of women who have worked in a male environment, whether in business or in the armed forces. They have developed the masculine side to behave like the men to compete for promotion and recognition. Then a crisis has occurred and they realize that they have suppressed a part of themselves. Many make the decision to leave organizations and spend time developing their feminine side. In the USA droves of people, especially women, have left the corporate world to find themselves again and the term 'downshifting' sprang from this.

Why is this important in developing our leadership gifts? It is clear that professional managers operate in a logical, rational way. As Tom Peters said, 'The numerative, rationalist approach to management dominates the business schools. . . . It seeks detached, analytical justification for all decisions. It is right enough to be dangerously wrong, and it has arguably led us seriously astray'.[32] This approach is very much the yang, and involves left-hand brain activity. It is this behaviour which is expected and rewarded, regardless of words such as values, vision and creativity being spoken.

This left-side thinking includes managers improving themselves through reading books, attending courses, research and projects. Most of our education system relies on left-brain learning. Yet inside every human being is a world of possibilities waiting beneath the surface. By the time we are adult we have experienced so much from life which shapes us and develops the personality. From this experience we can use intuition and creative ideas, and take leaps into the unknown. All of this comes from the right side of the brain, which is perceived in the rational world as 'woolly' and 'female stuff'. Some executives do exercise this intuitive part of the brain but do not usually admit it to colleagues. That is changing as Goleman's work has shown the importance of emotional intelligence, which is right brain activity, and now people are being encouraged to use this as its value has grown.

To be whole individuals and express our unique leadership gifts, we have to develop the yin and right brain activity. This includes intuition, knowing what the future will look like; feeling our way forward, not just planning; and living as being part of an interconnected world. Each of us will use our gifts differently. I use it when I am driving to a new place. I have my route planned but sometimes the road signs are not enough, so I use my intuition and feel which way is right. All I can say is, unlike the road signs, this is always 100% accurate for me.

Every human being has more potential than they know and as leaders this has to be developed. As a leader, you begin by seeing your own potential first then you will see others as leaders with unique gifts too. Kouzes and Posner wrote: 'Leadership is not the private reserve of a few charismatic men and women. It is a process that ordinary people use when they are bringing forth the best from themselves and others. When we liberate the leader in everyone, extraordinary things happen'.[33]

Every human being is born with leadership gifts. Leadership is not a matter of 'style' or charisma or management techniques; it is a daily quest for self-knowledge, understanding of the world, and fulfilling a purpose and self-actualization. The search for leaders is a search for human endeavour in every individual.

Summary of Essence 2

1. Are leaders special people who have around them power, riches, superiority and status?
2. Looking outside has created a helpless attitude of waiting for a hero or heroine to come and put everything right.
3. True leadership is about creating a domain in which we continually learn and become more capable of participating in our unfolding future.
4. Everyone can be a leader.
5. Leadership should be based on integrity and purpose beyond selfish desires.
6. Every human being has more potential than they know and as leaders this has to be developed.

Essence 3

Leadership is not the latest 'fad'. It is a timeless concept which has been recorded and studied for over three thousand years and gives us a richness of understanding.

Researchers today often ignore the considerable insights and ideas of the early attempts to understand leadership and, in doing so, miss out. For leadership has been a phenomenon since the emergence of civilization and a concept studied since then. As Bernard Bass says, 'Leadership is one of the world's oldest preoccupations'.[34]

In Egypt there were hieroglyphs for 'leadership' and 'leader' written about 5000 years ago. In the Instruction of Ptahhotep, around 2300 BC, the Pharaoh was regarded as having three qualities: 'Authoritative utterness is in thy mouth, perception is in thy heart, and the tongue is the shrine of justice'.[35]

In China, Confucius asked leaders to set a moral example in how they lived. He said: 'If you set your mind toward morality, your people will become moral. The character of the ruler is like the wind, and that of the people, grass. The grass bends when the wind blows upon it'[36] — a leadership lesson for those ruling countries today.

Service and leadership

In the 6th century BC Lao-tzu compiled his book *Tao Te Ching* or *How Things Work*. He wrote: 'leadership is service, not selfishness. The leader grows more and lasts longer by placing the well-being of all above the well-being of self alone'.[37] Taoism, as it is called, was about enabling people to become the best they could so that *they* achieve themselves.

The concept of delegation has been around for a while but Lao-tzu already had guidance on this for leaders everywhere. 'The wise leader does not intervene unnecessarily. The leader's presence is felt, but often the group runs itself. Lesser leaders do a lot, say a lot, have followers, and form cults. Even worse ones use fear to energize the group and force to overcome resistance . . . Remember that you are facilitating another person's process. It is not your process. Do not intrude. Do not control. Do not force your own needs and insights into the foreground. If you do not trust a person's process, that person will not trust you'.[38] There is so much here we can learn from in how we run organizations today. We talk of 'learning organizations' but can hierarchies with separate functional departments learn?

The ancient Greeks explained leadership through their stories of heroes such as Homer's *Iliad*. Later, Plato wrote of the ideal state and ideal leader. Here the leader would run good government, be educated and rule with order and reason. For Plato only a few should be leaders. 'There will be discovered to be some natures who ought to study philosophy and to be leaders in the State; and others who are not born to be philosophers, and are meant to be followers rather than leaders'.[39]

Virtue in leadership

Plato's pupil Aristotle was saddened by the lack of virtue among those who wanted to be leaders and said there was a need to educate young people for leadership. In *Politics* Aristotle wrote: 'But since we say that the virtue of the citizen and ruler is the same as that of the good man, and that the same person must first be a subject and then a ruler, the legislator has to see that they become good men, and by what means this may be accomplished, and what is the end of the perfect life'.[40] The education of young people still involves this challenge today.

At the time of the Renaissance, Machiavelli wrote *The Prince* which is still considered an insight into leadership. He believed leaders should be steady and firm, and should maintain authority, power and order in government. Machiavelli believed it was better to succeed with the popular support of people, but if not, then deceit, threat, treachery and violence were required. In England, Shakespeare showed leadership in all its human facets in his plays.

In Germany, during the 1830s philosopher Hegel believed that any leader should first serve as a follower so that they would understand their followers. He believed this understanding was crucial for effective leadership. This is still a principle used in the British Army and West Point in the USA today.

Modern theories

During this century we have seen situational leadership, trait leadership, theory X and theory Y, functional leadership, leadership styles, transformational leadership, servant leadership, values leadership and white rapids leadership.

Trait leadership was grounded in the assumption that some people are 'natural' leaders because they have certain characteristics not possessed by others. Hundreds of trait studies were carried out during the 1930s and 1940s. However, the findings were disappointing and the only conclusion that this extensive research could offer was that leaders are slightly taller and slightly more intelligent than other individuals!

In 1940, situational theory was put forward:

Leadership is specific to the particular situation under investigation. Who becomes the leader of a particular group engaging in a particular activity and what the leadership characteristics are in the given case are a function of the specific situation. . . . There are wide variations in the characteristics of individuals who become leaders in similar situations and even greater divergence in leadership behaviour in different situations. . . . The only common factor seems to be that leaders in a particular field need and tend to possess superior general or technical competence or knowledge in that area. General intelligence does not seem to be the answer.[41]

During the 1970s, John Adair took his ideas from teaching at Sandhurst into the wider world. His theory, known as functional leadership or action centred leadership, was based on three areas: the task, the team and the individual. The leader actively maintained all three. It suited many men but women found it a bit alien. Is this because women express their leadership gifts differently?

Also during the 1970s the first work was developed on leadership styles, with four distinct behaviours: supportive leadership, directive leadership, achievement-oriented leadership and participative leadership. Later came Blake and Mouton's four styles, which have been popular in training programmes.

Situational leadership raised itself again with the model developed by Blanchard. This is based on both leadership style and the development level of subordinates. The idea is that employees move forward and backward along a developmental continuum which represents their competence and commitment. The leader has to diagnose where subordinates are on the development continuum and adapt his or her leadership style to match this development level. The different styles are directing, coaching, supporting and delegating. Therefore, a leader has to be flexible in his or her style. Trainers in leadership like this because it is a useable and credible model.

Warren Bennis has written many books on leadership. His premise is that leaders are characterized by four key abilities:

- the management of attention, which means they create a compelling vision;
- the management of meaning, which involves communicating the vision to produce action;

- the management of trust, which demands consistent behaviour and remaining at the heart of things;
- the management of self, which evolves around self-understanding, persistence and resilience in taking the vision where it has never been before.

This work was based on people at the top of organizations or those who had achieved remarkable goals. Yet do all leaders do these things?

Stephen Covey sees leadership as having principles that apply to life, work and home. It is about accomplishing what you set out to achieve while living to certain principles, and self-awareness is part of this.

With constant change beginning in the late 1980s it is no surprise that the 1990s saw the rise of 'transformational' leadership. This involves assessing followers' motives, satisfying their needs, and treating them as full human beings. The concept was developed by James MacGregor Burns (1978) in his Pulitzer prize-winning book *Leadership*. It distinguished two types of leadership: transactional and transformational. According to Burns, transformational leaders are people who fundamentally alter the institutions they lead, as opposed to transactional leaders, who merely maintain or manage what they are given.

Transformational leadership involves motivating followers to do more than expected by raising their levels of consciousness about the importance and value of specified goals, getting followers to transcend their own self-interest for the sake of the team or organization, and moving followers to address higher level needs.

In the 1980s Bass expanded and refined transformational leadership. According to Bass transformational leadership consists of four behavioural components: charisma, inspiration, intellectual stimulation and individualized consideration. Here, the behavioural components of leadership interact to affect the followers' level of awareness and motivation. Transformational leaders raise the perception of the work objectives and task outcomes while elevating followers to their best. Therefore, the needs for achievement and self-actualization are higher than the need for security, for example.

One of the studies of transactional and transformational leadership caused a huge ripple in the development of leadership theory because it included gender. The work was undertaken by Judy Rosener. Here transactional leaders motivate people by carrying out transactions with them – by exchanging rewards for their services. The transactional leader articulates clearly what is expected of subordinates and identifies the rewards related to the performance for specific tasks. Transactional leadership provides control to the leader, who uses the self-interest of the follower in motivating follower performance.

Transformational leadership motivates by empowering followers, by transforming the self-interest of employees into the achievement of organizational goals. The transformational leader is concerned with expanding the awareness of the follower beyond his or her self-interest, empowering subordinates by appealing to intrinsic rather than extrinsic rewards.

Rosener found that men and women in the study used both leadership styles; however, the women were more transformational than their male peers. This is consistent with the belief that women feel more comfortable empowering others and encouraging team decision making than with directing subordinates via formal reward in exchange for performance. This is also consistent with the belief that men are socialized to compete as individuals, to see a direct connection between effort and reward, and are comfortable using direct control.

The research found no difference in the way women leaders and their male peers perceive the way in which subordinates follow them. However, it was found that women who described themselves as more feminine and males who described themselves as more masculine reported higher levels of female 'followership'. In other words, women tend to follow women who are seen as feminine and males who are seen as masculine. Perhaps they feel more comfortable with behaviour consistent with sex roles.

The study included how leaders use five power sources: coercive, expertise, referent (personality), reward and legitimate (position or authority). Rosener found that women leaders used referent power – charisma and contacts – more than their male peers. This is based on personal power rather than structural or authority power. In addition, women transformational leaders tend to use referent, expert and reward power, whereas male transformational leaders use only referent and expert power.

Women transactional leaders use only coercive power, whereas male transactional leaders use coercive, referent, reward and legitimate power. The findings imply that women tend to rely on more sources of power when they are transformational than when they are transactional. Conversely, men tend to rely on more sources of power when they are transactional. Finally, the female transactional leader is probably the worst model, alienating both female and male colleagues.

So, from this study on transactional and transformational leaders it appears that women are more likely to be transformational. This is important as few leaders can depend on titles and authority to motivate people today.

Organizational loyalty is at a low ebb and leaders who rely solely on self-interest and control by reward and punishment will become less and less effective. This is especially so as traditional hierarchies are being replaced with teamwork and interrelationships.

Other gender writers explain why the findings above are important with the change in organizations and more women in the workplace. Nancy Kline writes that women are taught from childhood that their excellence as women will be judged by the way they interact with people and by whether or not people flourish in their care. In comparison, Kline says that men are taught that their excellence as men will be judged by the way they control people, how well they promote themselves and by whether or not they stay 'on top'.

Kline believes that these two ways of thinking create different kinds of leaders. The first is controlling leaders, whereby leaders keep people from thinking and their purpose is to herd others. The second is interactive leaders, who ignite people's thinking and whose purpose is to launch others. Kline concludes that women's ability to think interactively is encouraged but not valued at present. There is strong evidence that the former, controlling leaders are many in number.

This is reinforced by a recent study from the Industrial Society,[42] which used a survey of 1000 employees. Bearing in mind that people are tied to the words and questions in a survey, the worst characteristics in the report came out as dogmatic, inflexible and inspiring fear. The survey focused on how others lead, especially those more senior to the person completing the questionnaire. The highest regarded attributes were the ability to delegate, trust employees with minimal supervision and actively encourage employee initiative. What is interesting is that these three attributes came above the ability to provide direction or take decisions. This is a strong message to senior managers whose inability to 'let go' is causing frustration and stress to employees.

A growing concept in the 1990s was 'servant leadership', as first described in 1977 by Robert Greenleaf. The servant leader concept focuses on the idea that leaders have the obligation to pursue service to others, rather than their own self-interest. This is very different to the 'fat cat boss' who gives himself huge pay rises even when the organization is not performing well.

Peter Block writes that 'when we choose service over self-interest, we say we are willing to be deeply accountable without choosing to control the world around us'.[43] Servant leaders are motivated not by what they can get from their positions but by what their roles as leaders allow them to give to others. Leadership is shared, not taken from people. Here, the doing becomes both greatness and goodness. Nowhere is this better demonstrated than in the corporate mission of the Japanese company Kyocera:

> Kyocera's management rationale is to provide opportunities for the material and intellectual growth of all our employees, and through our joint effort, contribute to the advancement of society and mankind.

All together in our history there is a richness of knowledge as we have tried to understand this human phenomenon called leadership. The writings of ancient time are as rich and worthy as those of modern times. Leadership has always been a part of human life. Leadership is everywhere. It is part of the human spirit and the reason why we have always searched for its meaning. Yet leadership is very much a personal expression, which leads to the next essence.

Summary of Essence 3

1. Leadership has been a phenomenon since the emergence of civilization and a concept studied since then.
2. Leadership is everywhere.
3. Leadership is part of the human spirit and the reason why we have always searched for its meaning.

Essence 4

To become a leader, you must become yourself.

The development of leadership is not about training people in 'what to do'. Leadership begins with being, not doing. As John Gardner said: 'It is our state of being and the development of the human spirit which is the real source of our ability to influence the world and effect positive change'.[44] In addition, the development of leadership is not the sole domain of those in human resource departments. Yet developing leaders has usually been given to this department. As Helgesen explains:

A great, almost urgent renewal of interest in the subject of leadership has characterized the last two decades. . . . Organizations seeking to adapt to a level and pace of change that can seem frightening and that is unpredictable have funded countless forums and workshops to instil leadership skills.[45]

On being a leader

But this is the management approach to developing leaders. Frances Hesselbein says:

The leader beyond the millennium will not be the leader who has learned of 'how to do it', with ledgers of 'hows' balanced with 'its' that dissolve in the crashing changes ahead. The leader for today and the future will be focused on how to be – how to develop quality, character, mindset, values, principles, and courage.[46]

James Bolt believes that conventional training does not work. He also states that learning leadership 'on the job' fails:

Most on the job development produces one-dimensional executives with overly developed quantitative and analytical skills. They have a narrow functional technical perspective as a result of spending their entire career in one area. They are often risk averse – afraid to make decisions – because of the grave consequences of making mistakes, and tend to mimic their bosses to ensure advancement. They often neglect family and friends in order to meet the demands of a system that too frequently encourages and rewards workaholism.[47]

How many times have you seen this?

Training alone is not sufficient in developing the leadership gifts of all. The key is for every individual to become a learner – including those working in HR. No one involved in training should train before they have been a learner themselves first and found their own leadership gifts. This involves learning about ourselves – who we are, our skills, prejudices, fears, talents, creativity and shortcomings. In other words, become a leader first, then help others find their leadership.

Teaching begins with serving

This is not done through 'training' only, but through using yourself in service to develop human beings who can discover for themselves their true nature and leadership potential. In other words, don't be a trainer or a lecturer: come out of the box and be a leader fulfilling a purpose and serving others. Lynne Twist, founder of The Hunger Project, wrote:

> To me, true service is an experience of wholeness, fulfilment, fullness, self-reliance, and self sufficiency for all parties – an experience of the magnificence and infinite capacity of human beings. When I'm really in service, I disappear. My identity is no longer present. I am one with he or she or that which I am serving . . .
>
> An act of service is an act of love and of trust. It's also an act of responsibility and of courage . . . a stand for the integrity of human life.[48]

Teaching others is a service, not a management function. It begins with respecting individual human beings and together taking an inward journey to explore their unique possibilities where you help them find their 'being'. This inner journey is necessary for everyone who wants to find their leadership. It includes facing our demons and fears, for left unchallenged, we will project them into the world and not become the leaders we are capable of being. Leadership is a personal journey of learning and lasts a lifetime.

Becoming yourself is an internal journey of both the mind and spirit. Reading books and attending conferences is a tiny part of it. By looking inwards there is a domain of possibilities waiting to be discovered. Just living as a human being gives experiences that are learning episodes. In your unconscious mind are events and feelings that influence your behaviour in everything you see and do.

Instead of becoming our true selves we fill ourselves with the outer world and what we can get. This is 'ego', which is concerned with 'I' and 'mine'. It begins early in our lives, enabling us to acquire our physical needs. Later it can grow to include the accumulation of money, status symbols, titles and recognition. The ego can give false or limiting beliefs to individuals about themselves which limits what they think they can achieve. It can result in passive behaviour, allowing others to control our life, or it can result in something as serious as an eating disorder. To search for our leadership and express it in the world, we have to rid ourselves of damaging ego to discover our true potential. When we become ourselves we become whole human beings with leadership gifts.

Summary of Essence 4

1. Leadership begins with being, not doing.
2. The development of leadership is not the sole domain of those in human resource departments.
3. Learning leadership 'on the job' often fails.
4. Training alone is not sufficient in developing the leadership gifts of all.
5. An inner journey is necessary for everyone who wants to find their leadership potential.

Essence 5

> *Leadership transforms the world.*

This is best described by Joseph Jaworski when he wrote that leadership is 'collectively listening to what is wanting to emerge in the world and having the courage to do what is necessary'.[49] Have you noticed when you sometimes get an idea, others also think of it, usually in another part of the world. This essence is very much right-brain activity. The key words are: 'what is wanting to emerge in the world'. It is 'knowing' where we are going. You cannot explain it scientifically because it is not left-brain activity. You just 'know'.

Knowing what needs to emerge

Fundamental to 'knowing' is keeping informed by reading, speaking to people, experiencing new things and learning. Most studies of leadership will tell you that learning is synonymous with leadership. To develop your leadership gifts you need to keep abreast of thinking in a variety of topics from science and technology to philosophy, or from ecology to economics. You need to understand how as a race of human beings, our knowledge is growing and how this impacts on how we see the world.

Jaworski says we 'collectively listen' which is more than hearing. It involves empathy and needs quiet where all 'noise' can be shut out. In this quiet, not only can you read and study, but you can hear the voice inside you which tells you ideas and knowledge of its own. Do not worry; this does not make you mad! All I know is that when you are quiet, you may sit and ask for an answer or some help with a problem. In the quiet you are always told what you ask for.

Learning to trust

This is a difficult part of leadership – trusting the universe. When we are busy achieving tasks we often forget that organizations are about relation-ships. The problem is that we have learned that relationships are risky – if you depend on someone, they may let you down; if you are honest with an individual, they may get angry so you avoid contact and so on. How often have you thrown yourself into work or tasks when a relationship has ended?

Connecting with others is a test of trust. In the same way, we need to trust the universe because we are connected to it. When we do this, we 'hear' what is wanting to emerge. We may call this trends, but it is actually much more. When you connect, you are not an isolated entity – you are part of the universe. As such, you become sensitive to its needs and what is emerging. It is as the physicist and philosopher David Bohm said: 'The individual's ability to be sensitive to that becomes the key to the change of mankind. We are all connected. If this could be taught, and if people could understand it, we would have a different consciousness'.[50]

Action

Finally, Jaworski says that we then need to act and do what is required. This action comes from courage, a word associated with moral strength. Integrity and morals have always been associated with leadership and inside every human being there is potential for these. The problem is when an individual allows life experiences to suppress them and their behaviour reflects their anger and pain. What prevents this happening in some people is an inner wisdom whereby individuals use their own understanding of the world rather than their conditioning from events in their lives. This essence is reflected in the behaviour and action of leaders. It begins with behaviour because transforming the world begins with transforming ourselves.

Summary of Essence 5

1. Learning is synonymous with leadership.
2. Before you find your leadership potential, you have to connect with the universe and place trust in it.
3. Transforming the world begins with transforming ourselves.

Essence 6

Individuals express their leadership gifts when they act as part of an integrated and interconnected whole as they fulfil their purpose and that of the organization.

Organizations themselves suppress leadership with their structures, processes and thinking. They are based on breaking everything up into parts and focus on getting the parts to work efficiently. It is interesting that one of the challenges for the Labour government in the UK has been to get senior civil servants and departments to cross-fertilize and work together more. One civil servant told me how frightened individuals were of this. But this tension is good, for it means that a new mindset is on its way.

Separate parts

As long as organizations break everything up into separate parts it is very difficult, if not impossible, for all employees to express their leadership. Instead, 'protectionist' behaviour is visible everywhere. At board meetings, directors protect their 'areas' with finance arguing with sales and marketing or information technology arguing with product development. At secretary level, PAs protect their bosses with avaricious telephone techniques and adding, 'He's so busy'. Flatter hierarchies with less bureaucracy are better but in many places have just resulted in fewer people doing more.

These structures go against human nature. Stephen Bergman and Janet Surrey found 'the primary motivation for all humans . . . [is] a desire for connection'.[51] Matter, which is a basic of life, is by its nature about connections and relationships with that around it.

A different structure

A different structure is required for leadership to be expressed by everyone. American author Sally Helgesen observed how some people, especially women, not only behaved differently in expressing their leadership but structured their organizations in a markedly different way. She was researching different ways of leading and observed:

> I noticed that the women tended to put themselves at the centers of their organizations rather than at the top, thus emphasizing both accessibility and equality, and that they labored constantly to include people in their decision making. This had the effect of undermining the boundaries so characteristic of mainstream organizations, with their strict job descriptions, categorizing of people according to rank, and restrictions on the flow of information.[52]

Helgesen went on to describe them as 'webs of inclusion' and found some men also structured in the same way, including an executive who left General Motors. She also found organizations outside business, including schools and a hospital, structured as webs.

A web or circular structure takes leadership away from the attachment of position. It allows a 'systemic' approach to work with fluidity and creativity abounding. Control is replaced with connectedness. Leadership can be expressed by every human being and learning becomes part of the day-to-day experience.

A web structure moves us away from seeing organizations as machines broken down into constituent parts. Instead the organization becomes a living entity with energy, which evolves and changes it shape as the different parts interact. Fundamental is relationships – both with people inside and outside the structure, and with the organization itself. The web structure takes us to the new era, leaving behind the remnants of the Industrial Age with its control and absence of the human spirit and creativity.

Helegesen says:

> Capitalism is evolving, like any living system. It needs to find ways of rejuvenating itself to get past inefficiencies that have become apparent . . . the very structure of Western technology has now come also to reflect the principles of life rather than reinforcing the image of the world as simply a giant machine governed by rigid and predictable laws.[53]

Organizations will change their structures when those within them change their consciousness. When this happens, leadership will thrive throughout. As part of the whole, leadership rather than management becomes the reality.

Summary of Essence 6

1. Individuals express their leadership gifts when they act as part of an integrated and interconnected whole.
2. A different structure is required for leadership to be expressed by everyone.
3. A web or circular structure takes leadership away from the attachment of position.

Essence 7

We are all leaders and followers at different times.

Someone who understood leadership and human nature was William Shakespeare. In his characters 'leaders' who happened to be born kings or queens were not necessarily leaders and vice versa. He also showed that even someone as strong as his Henry V was at times leader and at other times a follower, reliant on his men who, when needed, showed their leadership gifts. There is no greater leader than Shakespeare's Henry V yet his greatness recognizes that he cannot win without his men and that he is also in their hands. He puts his life in their hands, saying:

> And you, good yeomen,
> Whose limbs were made in England, show us here
> The mettle of your pasture; let us swear
> That you are worth your breeding: which I doubt not;
> For there is none of you so mean and base,
> That hath not noble lustre in your eyes.
> I see you stand like greyhounds in the slips,
> Straining upon the start. The game's afoot:
> Follow your spirit; and upon this charge,
> Cry 'God for Harry! England and Saint George!'[54]

Leaders and followers together

Leaders and followers are connected. You will be leader and follower at different times. In recent times, the British Queen has been perceived as a leader, but she was a follower just after the death of Diana, Princess of Wales when she followed the thoughts and feelings of the public and lowered the flag at Buckingham Palace and bowed to the coffin during the funeral procession. It is vital to know when to be a follower and when to express your leadership.

This essence may be difficult to accept when the perception of leadership in society is based on position, on top or out in front, knowing more than anyone else and having qualities which others lack. It is similar to the perception of seeing and believing that there is only one world – *the* world – and each of us is alone on that world. Yet as Maturana and Varela show: 'The world everyone sees is not *the* world but *a* world, which we bring forth with others'.[55]

Change of mind

When you realize how interrelated we all are it is easier to accept that we are both leaders and followers. It requires a change in thinking but this will happen. In *Global Mind Change*, Willis Harman asserts that when historians look back at the twenty-first century they will say that the most significant change was the change of mind. This will spread throughout society and will include our understanding of leadership.

Summary of Essence 7

1. We are all leaders and followers at different times.
2. Leaders and followers are connected. It is vital to know when to be a follower and when to express your leadership.

These are the seven essences of leadership:

- Leadership is distinctly different to management and is not just something to be added on to the job of a manager.

- Everyone is born with some gift of leadership, be it great or small. It is part of the human spirit and should be expressed in the world.
- Leadership is not the latest 'fad' but a timeless concept that has been studied and recorded for over three thousand years in an attempt to understand this human phenomenon. We should use this abundance of knowledge.
- Leadership starts with the individual and requires a journey of becoming your true self. This requires knowing and understanding who you are. Leadership begins with being.
- Leadership requires us to understand and listen to what is emerging in the world, share these experiences with others by connecting and then act accordingly. This is the transforming part of leadership.
- Leadership is expressed by everyone when people are connected and part of the whole rather than in separate components of a machine organization.
- Finally, leadership is about being followers as well as leaders; position or privilege is not what makes a leader.

A challenge

These essences leave us with a challenge. The present crisis in leadership in all walks of life is one of perception. We still see leadership as position and for the few. Our hierarchical organizations and management ethos propagate this perception. Those who have benefited from the past and present will resist changing. But change is already happening. Individuals are coming together to change the world. They are saying 'We've had enough of damaging the environment, buying foods which are not healthy, seeing people in poverty, putting our lives at risk when we travel because individuals are more interested in profits and self-interest'. The problems of the world are human failures. They begin with an individual. Resolving human failures requires change. It begins with an individual. Hermann Hesse wrote: 'To change the world, change yourself'.[56]

Every human being has some gift of leadership. It is a failing of humanity that most never know what it is. If we want the world we desire everyone has to participate, take responsibility and become the leader they are capable of.

The search for leaders is not about finding a few 'good', 'strong' individuals; the search for leaders is about releasing the potential which is in every human being. For those reading this book, it may begin here or it may be part of a journey you have already begun. To help you on your journey take with you this knowledge. Together, we will now travel through three circles which will help you find your unique leadership gifts. We will continue the journey in search of leaders.

3

The Transcendent Circle

At the centre of your being you have the answer; you know who you are and you know what you want.

Lao-tzu

Most of us spend our lives busy doing things. We rush to meetings, drop the children off, run to catch a train, help a colleague with a work problem, dash into the supermarket for food, try to finish off the important report through copious interruptions and so on. Yet to discover your leadership gifts, the first step is to *stop doing*.

There are many leadership programmes that will tell you what leaders *do*. Some will even put this into a list. They will then tell you that if you do these things, you too will be a leader. So you return to work with a list of good intentions which somehow never get the results you hoped for. Why is this? The answer is that the search for leadership begins with an inner search to discover *who you really are* and this is only achieved when you stop *doing* for enough time to *be*.

Transcend to be

Warren Bennis says: 'becoming a leader is synonymous with becoming yourself. It's precisely that simple, and it's also that difficult'.[1] There are no quick-fix training courses or techniques to enable you to be a leader – it is already within you if you will stand in silence and listen to your very being. Kouzes and Posner said: 'The quest for leadership is first an inner quest to discover who you are'.[2] We do this by first stepping into the transcendent circle.

The Circular Leadership Journey: The Transcendent Circle

To transcend means to rise above. In this context it is described by Susan Jeffers: 'Most of the time, we are immersed in fog and heaviness, not understanding that all we have to do is learn how to fly above the clouds'.[3] In other words, we need to stop rushing around and take some time to focus on becoming who we are capable of; to transcend and realize who we are as a leader. Think of it as allowing g force to take you up as if you were one of the RAF Red Arrows. By doing so, we can achieve so much more than doing a job or living a life that is dissatisfying. Stephen Covey wrote: 'The deepest part of human nature is that which urges people – each one of us – to rise above our present circumstances and to transcend our nature'.[4]

Who am I?

When we only wear a job label such as manager we only see the job, not the person as a whole human being with leadership gifts. These gifts are usually stifled at work through organizational structures and management processes. We get caught up in rushing around because it often makes us feel important, as well as having to deal with heavy workloads. Alan Briskin says: 'We are pulled in so many directions that the inevitable cry from within is "I can't find me." But who is the I and who is the me?'[5]

To discover this there is no doing in this central circle, only being. Meister Eckart said: 'People should not consider so much what they are to *do*, as to what they *are*'.[6] It is where to discover who you really are, all that makes you a unique human being. While we are rushing around doing, we forget how unique each human being is, including ourselves. Kay Gilley wrote: 'Leadership can and does occur at all levels in organizations; it emerges when people have the courage to incorporate the few simple truths of being into their whole lives'.[7]

Dead wood

When this doesn't happen, those running organizations or managing in parts of them create a 'slow death' for employees. There is a story about management guru Peter Drucker which puts this point across. He was speaking to a group of senior executives and asked them to raise their hands if there was a lot of 'dead wood' in their companies. Many in the audience raised their hands. He then responded: 'Were the people dead when you interviewed them and decided to hire them, or did they become dead wood?'[8]

We are not meant to become dead wood. We are in fact born to become who we truly are – if we allow ourselves to be. Kahlil Gibran wrote: 'Your daily life is your temple and your religion. Whenever you enter into it take with you your all'.[9] Life should be about the full expression of who you are. Is this how you live your life? If not, why? Only you can change it and it begins in this part of the circle.

Introducing Sisyphus

There is a Greek myth which tells the story of Sisyphus, who is condemned to roll a rock to the top of a hill, to see it roll back to the bottom, then roll it back up the hill to the top, where again it rolls back down, and so on through eternity. Week in, week out, day in, day out, Sisyphus worked. There are many such individuals today who work like this. Does your life feel like this? If you told Sisyphus to stop, his first reaction would be surprise, then relief, and then to start looking for something to do. This is because, like many, Sisyphus looks only outside for purpose. Like many, Sisyphus will never know what is inside him for while he is so busy he never has to confront his inner being.

In a world of fast continuous change and unpredictability we need courage to take leaps into the unknown and this is only possible when we know that *all we need is within us*. We all have leadership gifts but we have to learn how to express them in the world.

This is what people like past South African President Nelson Mandela, astronaut John Glen and scientist Marie Curie all had to do. What would the world be if these individuals had not taken their whole selves into their lives, decided to 'play safe', and not use their unique leadership gifts? The answer is straightforward for psychologist Abraham Maslow, who said: 'If you deliberately set out to be less than you are capable of, you will never truly be happy'.[10] He called this the Jonah Complex – the tendency within each of us to try to run away from our greatness, to not accept the challenge we hear coming from within us. This refusal to face up to our capacities for tremendous achievement and changing the world is something each one of us has to fight against.

Never have I heard this explained so clearly as in the book *A Return to Love* by American author Marianne Williamson:

Our deepest fear is not that we are inadequate.
Our deepest fear is that we are powerful beyond measure.
It is our light, not our darkness, that most frightens us.
We ask ourselves, 'who am I to be brilliant, gorgeous,
talented, fabulous?'
Actually, who are you not to be?
You are a child of God. Your playing small doesn't serve
the world.

There's nothing enlightened about shrinking so that other
people won't feel insecure around you.
We are all meant to shine, as children do.
We were born to make manifest the glory of God that is
within us.
It's not just in some of us; it's in everyone.
And as we let our own light shine, we unconsciously give
other people permission to do the same.
As we are liberated from our own fear, our presence
automatically liberates others.[11]

It takes courage to look within ourselves and discover who we are and
what leadership gifts we can offer the world. You know in your heart that
the relationship you have with yourself affects all others. For example,
when we doubt ourselves it is difficult to trust others. Courage is when
we look fear in the face and learn from it. Fear can be a teacher as well as
an adversary. Fear can be powerful – but only when you allow it to be.

Fear as a teacher

Oprah Winfrey told a story on her television programme about how
when she admitted on live broadcasting certain things in her past, fear
overcame her at the thought of what the tabloids would do. As it was,
her openness and honesty enabled viewers to relate to this woman.
Afterwards she said: 'What I learned from it, is the thing that you fear
the most, truly has no power. Your fear of it is what has the power. But
the thing itself cannot touch you. What I learned that day is that the
truth really will set you free'.[12]

Our fears are part of us and are there for us to learn. In *Crisis Points: Working through Personal Problems*, Julian Sleigh explores the notion of looking at the demons of our lives that make 'us shrink in fear and revulsion'[13] as bearers of gifts hidden under their wings. 'If we challenge them and make them yield up their gifts', he says, 'they will be satisfied and fly away, leaving us to benefit from what they brought'.[14]

Fears are usually connected to and related to our past. The key is not to let the past dictate our lives in the present. Bennis writes: 'we have the means within us to free ourselves from the constraints of the past, which lock us into imposed roles and attitudes. . . . We become free to express ourselves, rather than endlessly trying to prove ourselves'.[15] How many of us are living our lives trying to prove our worthiness to parents and teachers? When we stop this, we become ourselves. This is a road I have travelled myself and know how different it feels when you free yourself from the past. As Bennis continues: 'Letting the self emerge is the essential task for leaders'.[16]

Force of the heart

At work, we can either operate out of fear and decide to let the system run us, or operate out of the best we are and assist the system to work for everyone. We *can* create a new workplace where leadership replaces fear. It is up to every individual because there is only ourselves. As John Gardner says: 'Our state of being is the real source of our ability to influence the world'.[17] For inside each one of us is a truth of who we are and its integrity shines through when we are with others. Managers often ask 'how can I inspire others?'. Kouzes and Posner answer this best: 'The true force that attracts others is the force of the heart. It is when you share what is in your soul that you truly move others'.[18] Yet we are not encouraged to be open in the workplace. This even applies for executives.

When working with boards of directors and senior executives, I often go through a process whereby they open up with themselves and each other in a totally honest way. Before we begin, the look of apprehension on the faces is very visible. As each person completes this, the relief and smiles visibly show a new-found freedom in facing a fear and being honest. They have often spent years playing a game around the board table – protecting their own territory and behaving through their fears instead of seeing the whole picture.

Individuals who are considered leaders in the world today are failing because they are not facing their fears and learning from them. These leaders in companies, governments, schools, the civil service, the professions and so on are suffering from deep insecurity and fears about who they are and their self-worth. So they cling to the illusion of power, status, control while inside they are afraid.

Need for approval

The problem is that leaders based on position in hierarchies tend to be extroverts who ignore what is going on inside themselves. They rise to positions of power by operating effectively in the external world, often to the detriment of internal awareness and understanding. These leaders look outside in the external world for approval. In doing so, they create organizations that deprive others of their identity as a way of dealing with their own unexamined fears.

Anthony De Mello describes this in his typical direct manner. 'You were given a taste for the drug called approval, appreciation, attention'.[19] He shows that receiving this drug began when we were small and continues:

> So we were given a taste of various drug addictions: approval, attention, success, making it to the top, prestige, getting your name in the paper, power, being the boss. We were given a taste of things like being the captain of the team, leading the band, etc. Having a taste for these drugs, we became addicted and began to dread losing them. Recall the lack of control you felt, the terror at the prospect of failure or of making mistakes, at the prospect of criticism by others. So you became cravenly dependent on others and you lost your freedom. Others now have the power to make you happy or miserable.[20]

Is this how leadership should feel? Of course not – this is not leadership, it is captivity, and captivity is highly visible in today's world. How often have you felt it? How often have you been driven to gain the approval of others? There are many fears – fear of failure, fear of losing a job, fear of a boss, fear of poverty, fear of being alone, fear of the unknown, fear of power, fear of change, fear of not being able to cope or fear of never being good enough. A self-fulfilling prophecy takes over and leadership gifts diminish because people cannot learn when they are afraid.

These fears can sometimes turn to hate. In not rectifying and understanding their inner selves, some individuals start blaming those 'out there' – the economic market, the government, the well off, people of a different race, globalization, a different gender, a different sexual orientation. In not dealing with the internal fears we have even killed those who have become 'the enemy', as in so-called ethnic cleansing around the world.

Facing our fears

We must each face our fears to live without them. I always remember speaking to Rebecca Stevens soon after she had reached the summit of Mount Everest in 1993. She was the first British woman to achieve this and, incredibly, this was the first big mountain she had climbed. I asked her what was the most important thing she had learned, to which she answered: 'Never to be afraid again. I faced my fears on that mountain and became aware of myself. I know I will never be frightened of anything else ever again'.[21] Imagine the freedom in knowing that. Another climber, Jim Whittaker, who was the first American to climb Everest, remarked: 'You never conquer the mountain. You conquer yourself. Your doubts and your fears'.[22]

Facing personal fear was illustrated in the *Star Wars* film *The Empire Strikes Back*, when Luke Skywalker was on the planet Dagobah with Yoda, his teacher. The young Skywalker has to go into a part of the forest and confront an image of his arch-enemy, Darth Vader. What he is actually confronting is a reflection of his own anger, confusion and fears. In movies as in life, strength comes from facing your fears. But you also gain more than strength. You end up feeling a peacefulness and joy from within, which has to be experienced to comprehend.

If we perceive the world as a hostile place, it will affect how we behave and live. When we realize that the world is in fact a wondrous place, we can treat each day with awe and gratitude. When difficult things happen, they are the challenges many of us experience, which enable us to grow from the inside.

Our choice

According to Julian Sleigh[23] we have three choices:

1. Ignore the fear and hope it will go away.
2. Try and live with it.
3. Look for the gift within our fear and benefit from it.

This is why leadership is associated with courage – not to fight battles on a field or at sea or in the air, but to have the courage to deal with our own fears. We need courage to create our personal vision and that of organizations. We need courage to challenge the status quo and take risks every day.

When we explore the meaning of courage, we find it comes from the word *coeur*, which means heart – the centre of our being. Joseph Badaracco and Richard Ellsworth describe courage as 'to do and say what one believes to be right, rather than what is convenient, familiar or popular'.[24] Courage, then, begins from inside and is the only way to rid ourselves of fears. These fears can include being afraid of losing a job, afraid of our boss, afraid we will not meet deadlines or afraid of what colleagues think of us. We need to realize that courage is a friend available to all of us.

Kay Gilley wrote: 'Courage isn't courage if we don't continue to look fear in the face, to accept that fear is with us, and to move forward'.[25] This is why training courses or university programmes that focus on developing skills to manipulate the external world propagate the denial of the inner being and with it the fears that rule us. The result may be the ability to write a better business strategy – but the individual has not discovered their leadership. As Gilley wrote: 'There is no bag of magic techniques to help us to be leaders. The magic lies in our being'.[26]

Twice born

Those who are actually expressing their full leadership gifts have stood in the transcendent circle and taken an inward journey. For some, the process was forced upon them through what Abraham Zaleznik calls 'twice born'. He argues that there are those for whom being born and making the journey from home and family to independence is relatively easy. Then there are others who suffer as they grow up, feel different, even isolated and so develop an elaborate inner life. As they grow older, they become truly independent, relying on their own beliefs and ideas.

For Zaleznik, these second-born individuals are inner-directed and have 'found' who they are. First-borns discover who they are from their parents and teachers. The story of the first Red Arrow was that of a first-born; the second Red Arrow team leader story was that of a second-born. Zaleznik believes the second-born are charismatic. Perhaps the most obvious twice-born is the story of Nelson Mandela, who began as a young rebel, went on to struggle with his inner being while in prison and emerged a leader for both black and white in a new South Africa.

Fortunately, we do not all have to go to prison to find our being. But it does require time and courage. As for being charismatic, this is often over-used to describe people. Kouzes and Posner wrote: 'Research showed that those who were perceived to be charismatic were simply more animated than others. They smiled more, spoke faster, pronounced words more clearly and moved their heads and bodies more often. They were also more likely to touch others during greetings. What we call charisma can better be understood as human expressiveness'.[27] In other words, just express yourself.

This first step in the transcendent circle is not an easy experience as so much of us has been 'conditioned'. Warren Bennis describes the challenge: 'By the time we reach puberty, the world has reached us and shaped us to a greater extent than we realize. Our family, friends, school and society in general have told us – by word and example – how to be. But people begin to become leaders at that moment when they decide for *themselves* how to be'.[28]

The freedom to become

Within each of us we have both the experience of the past, including our childhood, and the capacity to shake off the past – if we are willing to. In searching for who we are we become aware of our powers and own belief in ourselves. With this discovery comes a freedom to become who we are capable of becoming. Margaret Wheatley explains: 'Life gives to itself the freedom to become . . . because life is about discovering new possibilities, new forms of expression. . . . Life is born from this unquenchable need to be'.[29]

This leads to real and sustainable transformation – the drug dealer who becomes a social worker or the abused child who becomes the wealthiest woman in the USA and is an inspiration for many. You are the only person who can empower you. The idea that managers empower people is wrong. What managers can do is create an environment for people to discover and practise their own power. But empowerment comes from within and from who you are. It means spending some time taking an inward journey, which is not easy. It is uncomfortable as we are not encouraged to do this. It means facing our inner thoughts and fears. It means questioning who 'I' is.

Anthony De Mello[30] asks thought-provoking questions like this: Can you know what 'I' is? You are a physical being, so is 'I' your body? Over seven years every cell in your body is replaced with a new one. The cells die but 'I' remains. You work in an organization and have a job title. Is 'I' your job description? Your job can be replaced or disappear, but 'I' remains. Is 'I' your name? You can change your name, but 'I' remains. We identify with labels such as I'm a Protestant or Catholic or Jew. Is your religious identity 'I'? Again, you can change this label, but 'I' remains.

Danah Zohar asks similar questions: 'Here am I, my body made of elements that once were stardust, drawn from the far corners of the universe to flesh out, however briefly, that pattern that is uniquely me, my soul a thing that can breathe in the enormity of such awe-inspiring origins. But who or what is this "I" that I think I am?'[31]

Trying to answer these questions, Zohar moves on to questions we have all asked ourselves at some time such as: 'Am I the same person as the shy, self-conscious teenager?' 'Am I the same person who married many years ago with little understanding of what commitment was?' 'Am I even the same person as the I who went to bed last night?'

There does seem to be a pattern that as we grow older part of us is still the little girl or boy and part of us is a different, new person. For those who follow a Buddhist view there is no 'I'. However, for Zohar there are several 'I's which overlap, thus making the self a highly integrated unity of many sub-unities. She writes: 'the "I" that we take ourselves to be, is real enough, but from moment to moment it is a shifty thing with fuzzy and fluctuating boundaries'.[32]

Leadership requires us to bring all these elements of who we are into the process of 'being' to become the leaders we are capable of. Throughout life your 'I' is developing and the experiences of living influence and change us. Some of you may be thinking: 'This sounds OK, but it is my boss who needs help to change'. What you are really saying is that even if I go through this process, it will not change anything because I cannot change my boss. So instead of taking any responsibility for yourself, you are passing it on to someone else. Therefore, you are not being honest with yourself.

Whoever looks into the mirror of the water will see first of all his own face. Whoever goes to himself risks a confrontation with himself. The mirror does not flatter, it faithfully shows whatever looks into it; namely, the face we never show to the world because we cover it with a persona, the mask of the actor. But the mirror lies behind the mask and shows the true face.[33]

Expressing your character

Within each of us is a persona and a character. Persona is a mask we create to protect ourselves from the external world and our own internal fears, whereas character is the essence of who we are and goes beyond what we do. You need to recognize when you are in persona or character for the two are different. When do you have difficult meetings? When does everything come together with ease and surprise you? Expressing your character goes beyond telling the truth – it demonstrates a total congruence between who you are and what you say and do. It happens when you express your authentic self.

Madonna was explaining how she had changed since the birth of her daughter in *USA Today*. 'I'm not re-inventing myself, I am going through the layers and revealing myself'.[34] When we stand in the transcendent circle we see all we were born with and who we are. Most important of all, we see our true authentic self.

The aim of this inner search is to know your deepest personal truth – your true authentic self. This integrity is what you will express in the world through your leadership gifts, which will require courage. Kouzes and Posner express this by saying: 'Integrity means we are living out of our inner wholeness and expressing it with congruence in our outer world. It's larger than honesty'.[35] Its power was visible when Ghandi won over the might of the British Empire. Mandela expressed it when he took over as President in South Africa without vengeance towards those who had kept him prisoner for much of his life.

Until we have stood in the transcendent circle and gone through an internal journey ourselves, we will never have the understanding that is so essential to use our leadership gifts in organizations, which are full of unique spirits, each finding their own expression. This realization enables us to see everyone we work with as unique spirits on their own journeys to discover their leadership gifts. As such, it becomes clear why the way we have 'managed' change has such a high failure rate. Real change begins with the individual, not the process or structure.

The dynamic urge

As human beings when we look inside to our very being there is something we find which is important to leadership called the 'dynamic urge', a term used by Robert Fritz. As human beings, we have various desires such as survival, love or accomplishment. Some arise from situations; for example, when getting lost on a mountain survival will be a strong desire. However, some desires are independent of situations and these are called the 'dynamic urge'. Fritz describes this dynamic urge as an 'intrinsic desire which is not tied to circumstances'.[36] Such desires are part of who we are and they are what makes us unique.

The dynamic urge is a genuine phenomenon of the human spirit in which people, no matter what their circumstances, continue to want to create something that matters to them. It is what has driven artists throughout history to spend days on a painting, foregoing food and company, until it is finished. It is what keeps entrepreneurs knocking on doors when they have had rejection after rejection. It is what keeps athletes training every day when they also have a full-time job and little financial support. It is in a teacher who never gives up on enabling the young students in an inner-city school even when the rest of the staff are full of scepticism and jealousy. We particularly see it expressed when people have had many knocks in life, been defeated, disappointed and hurt, yet still try to reach their aspirations and goals. We all know real-life stories that demonstrate this.

In cinemas around the world 'May the force be with you' is more truth than fiction now that we understand this part of the human species. It also partly explains why these books and films are so popular. They touch a part of the human side which is in all of us. Our behaviour as individuals can be explained when we understand this internal force and teleological drive. This force is in everyone, be it small or great. In *The Prophet*, Gibran explains:

In your longing for your giant self lies your
goodness: and that longing is in all of you.

But in some of you that longing is a torrent rushing
with might to the sea, carrying the secrets of the
hillsides and the songs of the forest.

And in others it is a flat stream that loses itself in
angles and bends and lingers before it reaches the
shore.[37]

For Abraham Maslow, this 'urge' is the need for self-actualization.
Maslow wrote: 'A musician must make music, an artist must paint, a poet
must write, if he is to be ultimately at peace with himself. What a man
can be, he must be. This need we may call self-actualization . . . It refers
to man's desire for self fulfilment, namely to the tendency for him to
become actually what he is potentially: to become everything that one is
capable of becoming'.[38]

The life force in everyone

What is clear is that each one of us has this 'drive' and in some it is
gentle, while in others it is a force that feels like a tornado. What is
being described here is 'spirit'. The dictionary describes spirit as the force
giving life to a body. When we stand in the transcendent circle we need
to become aware of that life force, an energy within us, for it is our guide
if we listen and as individuals we all have one. If as a group of human
beings we want to create the world we all desire, we have to begin here.

Margaret Wheatley said: 'We can create the lives and organisations
we desire only by understanding the enlivening spirit in us that always
is seeking to express itself'.[39] W. Edwards Deming, whose work on
quality fell on deaf ears until he went to Japan, concludes in his final
writings that quality is about the human spirit. He believes that as we
grow to understand that spirit, we will create organizations of quality.
How do we understand spirit?

Kay Gilley answers: 'We do not learn about spirit with our brains. We were born with spirit. . . . We learn by listening and being very still. We learn by breathing deeply and letting go of all the negative thoughts that clutter our minds with fear'.[40] She believes that until we have experienced this process we will not have the understanding required to be a leader in an organization that is full of unique spirits, each taking their own journey. It is this spirit or force which is missing in most organizations today.

Maslow believed this force to be linked to creativity and that the potential is everywhere because it is part of our being. He wrote: 'My feeling is that the concept of creativeness and the concept of the healthy, self-actualizing, fully human person seem to be coming closer and closer together, and may turn out to be the same thing'.[41]

The need for creativity

Organizations everywhere are coming to realize they need creativity and are focusing on trying to find the rare individuals who express it. What they should be doing is identifying the things in organizations that kill creativity. Maslow wrote:

> The key question isn't 'what fosters creativity?' But it is why in God's name isn't everyone creative? Where was the human potential lost? How was it crippled? I think therefore a good question might be not why do people create? But why do people not create and innovate?[42]

A study was conducted at Harvard University[43] several years ago which set out to measure IQ and spatial, visual, social and emotional intelligence of infants and young children. The researchers found that up to the age of four, the young children were up to genius level. After this age, through the development process, their scores were lower. What seems to happen is that after the age of four we are discouraged from showing our natural tendencies to creativity by parents, teachers and society. We are told not to approach a problem in this way, we should not do this and we should not do that.

Schools do not develop imagination, and companies prevent people from trying things and taking risks. The consequence is that by the time we are middle aged, our creativity is covered over and we fail to see beyond structure and order. But that creativity is still there, deep inside. The best description of creativity comes from Margaret Lulic when she says: 'Creativity is not being able to use every colour in the spectrum. It is about having only two colours and making miracles with them'.[44]

When you see something really beautiful – a view, a painting – everything stops and you look in wonder; this is a glimpse of your creativity. The problem is that we don't do this enough – especially in our busy working lives. John Gardner said: 'The highest levels (of creativity) can be expected in those lines of endeavour that involve man's emotions, judgement, symbolizing powers, aesthetic perceptions and spiritual impulses'.[45]

We each need some creativity in our lives as part of what we do every day. For too long creativity has been kept separate from intellectual or practical skills, just as intelligence has been separated from emotion. In the same way that Daniel Goleman showed us the importance of emotional intelligence, there is a need for creativity to be part of our lives because it feeds part of our inner being. While in the transcendent circle decide how you can feed and express your creativity and make time for it in your life, for creativity is part of your leadership.

Kouzes and Posner, in their wonderful study of leadership *The Leadership Challenge*, said that leadership was in fact an art: 'And in the art of leadership, the artist's instrument is the self. . . . Ultimately, leadership development is a process of self-development'.[46] This is why it is necessary to stand still in the transcendent circle first. As you work through this process you can start letting go of your petty self-interests. You can discard the weight of negative forces holding you down and transcend to becoming a leader.

Learning through accommodation

In the transcendent circle you are beginning to experience a form of learning that Jean Piaget called 'learning through accommodation'.[47] Throughout the three circles this is the process you will experience. It means that the change will come from inside you and enable you to understand the changing environment and be part of that changing world. It is as Arie de Geus explains: 'Our individual behaviour can be explained only by understanding the internal force of our goals and teleological drive, together with the forces coming from the outside environment'.[48] When we are busy doing, we are not learning as we should be.

Gib Akin from the University of Virginia says that there are two motivations for learning. The first stems from a need to know, like a thirst or hunger for knowledge. The second motivation is based on individuals' sense of themselves and the gap they are aware of in what they are and what they should be. Which one of these motivations drives you? Are both a factor?

Values

Having explored who you are as a complex, unique human being there is one final step which when completed will take you to the next circle in the spiral. All that you are as a human being is held together by your values and beliefs. It is time to explore those values which hold you together. These values should be seen in everything you do, for these moral principles come from your consciousness deep inside your being.

After years in prison, the Czech leader Vaclav Havel addressed the US Congress in 1990.

the salvation of this human world lies nowhere else than in the human heart, in the human power to reflect, in human meekness and in human responsibility. Without a global revolution in the sphere of human consciousness, nothing will change for the better in the sphere of our being as humans, and the catastrophe toward which this world is headed – be it ecological, social, demographic or a general breakdown of civilization – will be unavoidable.[49]

We need to be aware of our deep conscious values, which should be expressed as part of our leadership gifts. When this happens, we will stop being the victims of this world and become its creators. We saw in Chapter 2, that moral behaviour is lacking in the world today where leadership is based on position. It is up to every human being to change that and to do so means becoming aware of these deep values in our consciousness.

The Greeks believed that integrity, honesty and moral behaviour were fundamental to leadership. However, this is not about seeking it in a few 'good' men or women with certain characteristics or traits because then they will be the only ones we will see it in. Rather, let us start from the viewpoint that we can find honesty in most people.

Maslow said: 'each of us is born with certain innate needs to experience higher values; just as we are born physiologically with the need for zinc or magnesium in our diet. . . . Every human being has the instinctive need for the highest values of beauty, truth, and justice, and so on'.[50]

Global values for today

Rushworth Kidder, President of the Institute for Global Ethics in the USA, took 'twenty four men and women of conscience', thought leaders from all parts of the globe, and asked them to decide what would be on a global code of ethics. They set out a menu of global values. As we look at these, think how each would change the world when expressed fully and then decide which you are passionate about and which you will express as part of your leadership.

Love

The first value was love, which is a feeling from inside and should therefore be expressed spontaneously. Roger Harrison discusses love in organizations expressed in the beauty and quality of products or services, in the comradeship of co-workers, in the loyalties between people. He also remarks that it is a word we dare not use at work because of the male chauvinism of business.

This value is very difficult for those individuals who have not been shown love. Children who go into care learn to become so self-sufficient they have great difficulty in feeling trust and love because of the way the 'system' moves them around. As soon as they get to know one safe home, they are moved again. This value is much easier to express as part of your being when you have been surrounded with love. If we can learn from hard times, we must also learn to love from gentle affection too. How can you express love in your leadership?

Truth

The second value was truthfulness or honesty. Here, the context is for every human being to integrate truth into who they are. When we do not see this in behaviour from people, we become distrustful and cynical. Therefore, trust and truth go hand in hand; you cannot have trust without truth. However, the first truth is to yourself and while in the transcendent circle you must come to know your authentic self. What makes you a unique human being?

What is interesting is that in every study undertaken on both sides of the Atlantic to establish what people want in leadership, honesty is always the most important. In other words, we desire honesty in the world and we should not accept less. However, it begins with ourselves. We cannot expect the world to be honest if we are not honest with ourselves and those around us. In the film *Excalibur*, Merlin is asked the question: 'What is the most important quality that a knight must have?', to which he answers: 'Truth. For when a person lies, they murder some part of the world'. How can you express truth in your leadership?

Fairness

The third value is fairness, which some see as equality. This is about treating every human being the same, where advantage of position or money is obliterated. Do you treat a stranger the same as a friend? This value has much work needed in the world today. Ligget-Stashower, a US PR company, used data to get a strong message across. It is a message about our world.

> If the world were a town of 1000 people, there would be 564 Asians, 210 Europeans, 86 Africans, 80 South Americans and 60 North Americans. 700 would be illiterate and 500 would be hungry.[51]

Margaret Lulic added to this: 'the largest industries, in terms of dollars, involve the sale of illegal drugs and weapons. About 250 people are consuming . . . 70% energy, 75% metals, 85% wood and they live in the north part of the town who are polluting the rest. This is the reality of the global picture'.[52] How can you use your leadership to change this unfairness?

Freedom

The fourth value was freedom. It is one of the defining values of humanity. Liberty demands a sense of individuality and the right to express ideas freely. Liberty is about the many, not the few. 'Without the principle of individual conscience, every attempt to institutionalize ethics must necessarily collapse',[53] said Oscar Arias, one of the 24 participants. 'The effect of one upright individual is incalculable. World leaders may see their effects in the headlines, but the ultimate course of the globe will be determined by the efforts of innumerable individuals acting on their conscience'.[54]

This is why raising people's awareness that everyone has some gift of leadership within them is so important. We are all responsible for freedom and the future of this planet. When standing in the transcendent circle we can look into ourselves and remember how much more we have achieved when we have had the freedom to act.

Unity

The fifth value was unity – to be part of an interconnected world. When we make this value part of our being we realize that the planet and its resources belong to all, not just the wealthy. We are one people made up of a richness of patterns and colours. Tarzie Vittachi of Sri Lanka told Kidder that by embracing unity there can be a global vision capable of taking humanity from 'unbridled competition to cooperation'.[55] This is what is demanded of us now: putting our community first meaning the earth first and all living things.

When we go on an inner journey into our being we realize that we are not alone, but rather part of something large. John Gardner wrote: 'Consciousness of the unity of all life lies at the heart of being. Yet we live in a reality that is fragmented and thus lose the energy of the whole'.[56] In the transcending circle think of all those around you who have helped you and guided you in your life so far. How can you express unity in your leadership?

Tolerance

The sixth value identified by the group was tolerance, which is respect for the dignity of each human being. When searching within yourself, ask what makes you intolerant. By the way, this is not impatience, but a stronger desire to hurt another human being. Most intolerance stems from fear. We now have to face those fears before leaving the transcendent circle. In facing all fears, we learn. From learning comes understanding and we move away from dogma. We should all make tolerance part of our leadership.

Responsibility

The seventh value was responsibility, without which we become powerless to act. In Confucius' thinking, not taking responsibility for yourself is regarded as shameful. In the West, our laws have taken away some individual responsibility, which we need to address. If someone is taken ill on an aeroplane and an individual tries to help, they can now be sued. Many doctors in the USA in particular are very aware of rules that undermine their desire to be responsible for others.

How many times have you been affected by someone saying 'I'm not responsible for that'. My experience of the public sector in particular, is of offices full of people not taking responsibility and 'passing the buck'. Taking responsibility begins with yourself. Life knocks us around, but how we react to those knocks is our responsibility. Look in your past and how you have dealt with responsibility. Now how can you express responsibility today?

Respect for life

The eighth value in the search for a global code was respect for life. Oprah Winfrey told *Harper's Magazine* one year that her Christmas wish was: 'that children be treated as people, and not as property; that their rights as human beings on the planet to food, shelter, education and health, be taken seriously'.[57] However, this does not only focus on human life, but includes every life form. If we respected life we would take greater care of animals and plant life, which sustain the balance of the planet.

This value often carries with it raw emotion as it can include issues such as the death penalty, euthanasia and abortion. These issues often bring with them the dogma of organized religions and intolerance, thus showing that values are not easy to express in the world. How will you express respect for life?

Learning

But there is a value missing that is equally needed in the world today – that of learning. It is through learning that we continue to evolve and live in a fast-changing world. Every human being should be given both access to learning and the opportunity to learn. It is part of becoming a unique human being with a part to play in the unfolding of life. Lifelong learning is much more than a government initiative and as such deserves to be added to these global values. How will you make learning part of your leadership?

These nine are worth exploring as part of your journey to being. However, do not get confused in seeing them as a list of qualities but rather values that need to be expressed in the world to help us all become the best we can be. To be a leader is to be a human being who appreciates other human beings. Do the 'leaders' in the world and in your place of work express this? As long as everyone relies on a few individuals who are hooked on power and self-interest the potential we have will never be realized. But if the leadership gifts of all people were expressed fully through the values expressed here we could make the world a wonderful place to experience our lives as human beings.

Kouzes and Posner wrote: 'You cannot lead others until you have first led yourself through a struggle with opposing values'.[58] The reason they give is thus: 'Without a set of such beliefs, your life has no rudder, and you are easily blown about by the winds of fashion'.[59]

When we begin by standing in the transcendent circle, taking an inward journey and completing it with a clear picture of who we are and who we can 'become' as leaders, then leadership has meaning in the world much greater than position, being the boss or taking command. Margaret Wheatley wrote: 'We can create the lives and organizations we desire only by understanding the enlivening spirit in us that always is seeking to express itself'.[60]

Leadership cannot be taught, only experienced and learned, and it begins with time in the transcendent circle. While there ask yourself some questions. They will help you stop focusing on what you *do* and begin to consider *who you are as a human being in community with others*.

Questions

Take a blank piece of paper and give yourself the space and time to ask yourself these questions:

1. What sort of person am I today?
2. What sort of human being do I want to be?
3. What drives me?
4. What is important to me, my values and priorities?
5. What have I learned about myself so far?
6. What am I going to do with this information?

You are now becoming a fully aware individual and ready to take the next step in search of your leadership. You are taking the first steps to transcend to what you can be. You are becoming aware of your being.

Robert Greenleaf at the end of *Servant Leadership* expresses his personal belief for humankind and the importance of awareness.

Awareness, below the level of the conscious intellect, I see as infinite and therefore equal in every human being, perhaps in every creature. The blinders which block our conscious access to our own vast awareness are the uncompensated losses we have sustained; and the errors we have acquired from our cultural inheritance, from the undigested residues of our own experience, and from our conscious learning . . .

Remove the blinders from your awareness by losing what must be lost, the key to which no one can give you but which your own inward resources rightly cultivated will supply. Then set forth upon your journey and, if you travel far enough, filling the voids of loss with the noblest choices, you *may* be given the secret of the kingdom: awe and wonder before the majesty and the mystery of all creation.[61]

It is time to travel to the middle of the spiral and the second circle.

4

The Translatory Circle

Leadership reflects a person's mindset and his or her approach to the world.

Noel Tichy

The Circular Leadership Journey: The Translatory Circle

*I*n the search for leaders you are now ready to stand in the second circle. Having taken an inward journey and explored who you are as a human being, the next stage is to journey into the external universe to understand the world in which you live. Each of us has a picture, a view of what that world looks like. That picture has changed as generations of philosophers and, later, scientists have lived and died. But they have left an impact on how people see the world today. Not all can be included here in one chapter, but their influences are present in those who are mentioned. In this circle you will see that an old worldview is causing problems in organizations today and suppressing leadership. Therefore, we need to understand how this worldview came about and what the new one will look like. We will do this by travelling through time. It is a long journey, but very important in understanding how we see the world and how this relates to the concept of leadership.

Understanding our human history increases our awareness of competing values and the way individuals, organizations and countries choose to operate. The more we know about the world, the easier it is to be confident within it. To become an effective leader a full understanding of the world is required. Max De Pree wrote: 'The first responsibility of a leader is to define reality'.[1] To do this requires a real understanding of how we have arrived at our present reality. Margaret Lulic wrote with wisdom: 'We each have acquired a set of beliefs and values, as well as a way of seeing things, that we believe is the truth or reality. If we forget that we ourselves and others created much of this reality, we lose our power to forge something different. If we remember this however, we will know we can create something else'.[2]

Even in the past fifty years our view of the world has changed as technology enabled us to see pictures of the Earth from space for the first time – a beautiful blue planet, so small in a huge expansive universe. These changing pictures of reality affect how we see ourselves in our world. Sometimes those changes are so immense that they change the way we see everything. They are what are called 'paradigm shifts'. We need to understand our world and these paradigm shifts to help us in search of our leadership, and we do that in the translatory circle.

Sisyphus joins us again

Our worldview or mindset describes how we perceive and filter in our minds information to make sense of the world. As human beings we are selective in what we observe and biased in how we interpret that information. Do you remember Sisyphus, whom we met in the first circle? Sisyphus was pushing a stone up a hill for eternity. How does he see the world? Hard, unfair, merciless? You can imagine him getting very bitter over the years until the bitterness becomes hate and anger. If one day, someone were to try to help him his behaviour might be cold and rude, so the helpful person would leave him to continue pushing stones. It is our perception of the world and ourselves that determines how we live, how we resolve things and how we behave.

To translate means to go from one language to another. But to do this the language has to have meaning. For meaning, there has to be understanding. In the translatory circle we are going to explore how we see the world and understand it as this will influence how you express your being and leadership in the world.

Making sense of reality

How we make sense of our reality and worldview has been through the influence of mainly men over thousands of years. To have knowledge and understanding of this is vital in the process of developing our thinking in the new millennium. Therefore, our journey in this second circle is a journey of history. However, history has often failed to record many of the great female minds so I am aware of their absence here.

In this circle, you will learn the story of how the 'world reality' has unfolded over time. It is a journey of both science and philosophy and of the endeavour for knowledge and understanding. German philosopher Hegel said that science without philosophy can have neither life, spirit nor truth. From a very different philosophical viewpoint, Bertrand Russell believed that science and philosophy were two related aspects of our knowledge of the world – a view I endorse, and my experience is that together they create a richness and synergy in understanding life. They both share the goal of exploring human experience and knowledge. Science grew from philosophy and a way of understanding this is to see philosophy as the mother and science as the son.

Philosophy, and in particular the thinking of the ancient Greeks, has always influenced modern science. However, just understanding the theories is not sufficient. You will see that in discovering the progression of theories about the world the individual theorist and his (or her) life influences were always present. In other words, there is no such thing as a totally objective enquiring mind, only wonder of the world we live in. So fasten your seat belt as we travel back in time – back thousands of years.

The human journey of knowledge

There is no doubt that where you live in the world influences how you understand that world. The greatest influence in understanding the 'Western' world came from the Greeks over 2500 years ago where learning was part of life for the well off. The Greeks had conquered a substantial part of the world and so their influence was significant.

What is the world made of?

The man regarded as the first of the Western philosophers was Thales in the sixth century BC. He asked: 'What is the world made of?' He believed that ultimately there must be one element. He believed this to be water. He was right in saying that there was one fundamental building block to all of life. We now know this to be energy. Even as long ago as Ancient Greece, there was an argument you can hear today. Parmenides of Elea in Southern Italy argued that in the world 'nothing changes' whereas Heraclitus of Ephesus in Asia Minor said that 'all is flux'.

If you thought atoms were a twentieth-century phenomenon you will be surprised to learn that the Greeks already had views on atoms. Leucippus and the Ionian Democritus suggested that the world was made up of tiny, invisible particles of eternal atoms that were different sizes and shapes, and in between them was void. Democritus also believed that the Milky Way was a discontinuous collection of thousands of stars. How do we know this? Democritus' ideas on atoms survived in the writings of a Roman poet called Lucretius in his work *De rerum natura*, a copy of which survived the Dark Ages and was found in 1417.

One of the ancient Greeks who has had a lasting impact on our understanding of the world and had a different view on atoms was Pythagoras, who set up a religious sect in Southern Italy. His followers were vegetarians and believed in the transmigration of souls.

Mathematics is everything

Pythagoras was born around 580 BC and he passionately believed mathematics was everything. This led to measuring the circumference of the Earth, which was believed to be round not flat – it took the rest of us much longer to realize this. He also linked mathematics to music and found that notes forming chords that sound harmonious could be worked out mathematically, which led to his universal theory of the 'harmony of the spheres', establishing the mathematical worldview. He and his followers distinguished 'number' or pattern from substance or matter, viewing it as something that limits matter and gives it shape. They asked: 'what is its pattern?' not 'what is it made of?' Pythagoras believed that the universe could be expressed mathematically and for him the atom was 'number'.

Eastern thinking

What is interesting is that around the same time Pythagoras was in the world, so too were Buddha and Confucius. Each tried to teach a way of living which was also pursued by followers. The key concept of Confucius' thinking was *ren* (*jen*), which translated means love – not the romantic love we might think of, but the highest virtue which comes from the heart and is developed through education and moral codes in all social institutions. In addition, the philosophy of Confucius says that an individual is not an isolated entity. Rather, an individual exists only in a set of relations with others. In fact, Confucius writes: 'In order to establish oneself, one has to establish others. This is the way of a person of ren'.[3]

The journey of mankind in which humanity reaches highest fulfilment was taught by Buddha. The religion he founded has spread around the world and is still growing today. In Greece others were also making their mark on the world.

The great teacher

Perhaps the most well-known Greek was Socrates, who believed that learning should be more about how humans ought to live rather than about how nature works. For him, virtue represented knowledge. As far as we know Socrates did not write anything but instead taught by word of mouth. He questioned everything, including the democracy of Athens. When Socrates asked a question such as 'What is justice?' he was not asking for a definition, he was looking for the character, or essence, of this word, which we use to mean just laws or just decisions. He was trying to discover the very nature of the word.

The questioning by Socrates encouraged people to question everything and it exposed the ignorance of those in power who were expected to know the answers. Above all, Socrates taught the importance of personal integrity.

Such questioning was disruptive to those in power, and Socrates was eventually accused of being too enquiring and charged with 'blasphemy' against the state religion. At his trial, he defended himself and from his speech we can see the goodness of this man:

> If you say to me, Socrates, Anytus fails to convince us, we let you go on condition that you no longer spend your life in this search, and that you give up philosophy, but if you are caught at it again you must die – my reply is Men of Athens, I honour and love you, but I shall obey God rather than you, and while I breathe, and have the strength, I shall never turn from philosophy, nor from warning and admonishing any of you I come across not to disgrace your citizenship of a great city renowned for its wisdom and strength, by giving your thought to reaping the largest possible harvest of wealth and honour and glory, and giving neither thought or care that you may reach the best in judgement, truth, and the soul . . .

> For it is my one business to go about to persuade young and old alike not to make their bodies and their riches their first and their engrossing care, but rather to give it to the perfecting of their soul. Virtue springs not from possessions, but from virtue springs possessions and all other human blessings, whether for the individual or for society.[6]

Socrates was found guilty. Given a choice between a fine and admitting his crime and taking his own life by drinking hemlock, he chose the latter. His enquiring, thinking and ideas had become a threat. But this did not frighten Socrates for he believed that by dying he would join other thinkers, as is recorded in Plato's *Apology*:

> Above all I shall then be able to continue my search into true and false knowledge as in this world, so also in the next. I shall find out who is wise and who pretends to be wise and is not. What would not a man give, oh my judges, to be able to examine the leader of the great Trojan expedition or numberless others. What infinite delight would there be in conversing with them and asking them questions. In another world they do not put a man to death for asking questions, assuredly not.[7]

The method of dialogue

Socrates established the method of dialogue – seeking truth by a process of question and answer. It is a way of enabling individuals to re-examine what they think they already know and is fundamental to the translatory circle of learning about the world and leadership.

Plato had been one of Socrates' pupils and his own writings gave a central role to mathematics again in understanding the world. He believed that the more we pursue our studies in physics, we will see that mathematical relationships are present in everything in the material world. Plato could be very hostile to the arts, which he saw as holding us back from understanding the world. He founded the Athens Academy and taught others.

Plato's most famous pupil was Aristotle, born in Macedonia. He entered Plato's Academy, where he studied politics, law, mathematics, astronomy and rhetoric. Later he was invited to become tutor to the future Alexander the Great. Having completed this, he returned to Athens where he founded the Lyceum. Here his work and writings were based on observation of forms and structures in the world, whereas Plato's emphasis had been on a source of form or structure *beyond* the world; this led to rationalism, treating reason as the basis for knowledge.

The foundations of science are laid

Aristotle mapped out for the first time the many fields of enquiry, including physics, logic, political science, economics, psychology, metaphysics, meteorology and ethics. He invented technical terms which we can hear today such as substance, energy, induction, essence, dynamic, property, category, proposition, accident, topic and universal. Aristotle collected data and his work consisted of categorization or codification of knowledge. He was laying the foundations of Western science.

During the Dark Ages, following the fall of the Roman Empire, knowledge of Aristotle's work died out in Europe, but was kept alive in the Arab world. From here it made its way back into Europe during the late Middle Ages and became the single body of quasi-scientific knowledge for Europeans.

There is one great difference between the Greeks and Western science: the Greeks' attempts to understand the world gave a picture or viewpoint of the world and wherever they conquered, they influenced; modern science not only gave a viewpoint but *changed* the world. Between both came a very different and enforced worldview – that of the Church. However, the contribution of the Greeks was to move understanding to rational explanation.

Christianity ties thinking to belief

Now began a time of conflict between the followers of the old pagan thinkers and the new Christian thinkers in the early centuries after the death of Christ. The early Christians were divided into two groups: those who told stories of Jesus and how he taught people how to live, and those who placed more emphasis on his death and resurrection, led by Paul. The latter would come to be the basis of the new religion, which required unquestioning belief and acceptance.

One of the victims of this was Hypatia, who with her remarkable intellect and personality taught in Alexandria lecturing on the works of Plato and Aristotle. She was highly regarded and possibly the most influential teacher in Alexandria, which attracted people from all parts of the Greek-speaking world. She was quite literally torn to pieces by a Christian mob, urged on by monks who opposed the 'pagan' ideas that she so successfully espoused. The church needed control and found the writings of Plato attractive because of its emphasis in hierarchy and authority. Therefore Christianity shaped our thinking of the world through a hierarchical structure and control through fear.

Christianity is not primarily a philosophy. Its beliefs are of a historical nature based on the belief that God made the world and then not only appeared but *lived* in the world as a man called Jesus in Palestine 2000 years ago. This life took a certain course, for which we have historical records.

Dark and light on earth

The overthrow of the Roman Empire under the onslaught of Barbarians such as the Goths and Vandals began the period known as the Dark Ages in Europe. The Germanic tribes that had destroyed Rome now invaded Britain but stopped at the Irish Sea. Ireland, home to Celtic Christianity, became a place of philosophical thinking and civilization. Also while this was going on, Islam flourished throughout what had been Alexander's empire and North Africa.

In China civilization reached its greatest period and was renowned for its poetry. In Japan, a distinctive culture was emerging. Europe eventually emerged from a thousand years of darkness and looked to the skies for understanding once again.

Centre of the universe

Ptolemy had been an astronomer who lived in Alexandria in the second century AD. His account of reality was that the Earth was at the centre of the universe while other planets circled around us. During the Middle Ages the Catholic Church incorporated this into its view of the world. Mankind had an arrogance that made him regard himself as supreme over other living things. The words 'made in God's image' were taken quite literally by the church. Ptolemy built a model to show his worldview but it was very flawed. However, this worldview was naturally supported by the Church and lasted for around 1500 years because the Church dominated people's thinking and funded all learning. Christianity replaced other belief systems in Europe and this model was used to reinforce its hold.

The Church believed that the use of force against dissenters was just. In 1478 the Spanish Inquisition was set up, which made it law that Moslems and Jews should convert to Christianity. This oppression led to individuals questioning the picture of reality.

By the sixteenth century, others were beginning to question Ptolemy's theory and one of these was the Polish churchman Copernicus who put the sun at the centre of the universe. The Church at the time did not see Copernicus as a threat and tended to ignore his work. They did not realize that such revolutionary thinking could become popular. But soon his ideas were becoming a concern for if his theory was right then the authorities (the Church and the Bible) were wrong. Not only this, but if they were wrong about this then they may be wrong about other things too.

A revolution in thinking

Could it be that humans were no longer the centre of everything and that everything else did not revolve around us? When this realization spread it had the shock of an earthquake and people began to question religion. Yet it was to become a way of thinking which others took up.

One of these other men was Copernicus' German follower, Kepler, a brilliant theoretical thinker. Kepler studied the skies and devised astronomical tables which enabled him to derive empirical laws on planetary motion. He saw patterns in everything. He believed, with the Pythagoreans, that God must have created a universe according to some simple numerical pattern and turned to geometry to try to unravel the pattern. The idea of a mechanical universe began to emerge, one which operated in accordance with laws that could be expressed mathematically and, though created by God, could be discovered by Man.

Copernicus believed that the motions of all heavenly bodies were circular and uniform, but Kepler showed otherwise. He demonstrated that the planets move in ellipses, not circles, and that their motions are faster in some parts of their orbit than in others. This destroyed the belief that all celestial movements must make symmetrical patterns, which had begun in ancient Greece and had acquired a religious basis in the Middle Ages. So more of the worldview was being smashed and the thinking being challenged.

Kepler supported the notion of the sun at the centre of our world and the reality became that our galaxy was the centre of the universe.

The Church still did not feel totally threatened until one of their own countrymen began to realize that his observations showed a different worldview to that propagated by Rome.

A genius changes our world

Galileo was a Professor of Mathematics in Italy and performed experiments to discover the laws of falling bodies or laws of motion. Born into a noble but poor family, he resisted his father's plans to study medicine and turned to mathematics. So began a remarkable intellectual life's work. He knew we moved with the Earth but could not explain why we did not fall off. Galileo built and used his own telescopes and believed that the Church's view of the world was not correct. Using the best of his telescopes, what Galileo saw convinced him that Copernicus was right – the sun is at the centre of the universe. He studied shadows on Venus which from their changing patterns, showed them to be from Venus orbiting the sun.

In 1616, the Church publicly denounced the work of Copernicus and told Galileo to abandon his work. He tried to persuade them otherwise and published his work but was arrested. The Church made him a prisoner for the rest of his life. Yet Galileo was a genius and his work includes so much of our reality. He discovered the principle of the pendulum, which transformed both the manufacture and accuracy of clocks. Fundamental was that everyone up until this time had believed that the heavier a body is, the faster it will fall. Galileo showed that all bodies fall at the same velocity regardless of their weight and as long as they are not interfered with by some other pressure.

He also discovered that heavenly bodies do not move naturally in circles or ellipses, but in a straight line unless some other force acts on them. Galileo also found that if several different forces act on a moving body at the same time, the effect on its movement is as if they had acted separately and successively. Throughout his life, Galileo remained a Christian but he knew that what people believed was not true and they had to be told.

Galileo's work would not be complete until our reality included how planets stayed in orbit and how we did not fall off the Earth. Galileo's work was finished when he was tried and condemned by the Inquisition, which put him under house arrest – such was the control of the Church over people's search to understand our world. Galileo said that those in power and authority, including the Christian religion, had no right to interfere with the truth-seeking activities of science. Like Socrates, he believed that knowledge was worth seeking even if it meant death or confinement.

Controlling nature becomes the goal

In England, the statesman Francis Bacon was also influencing people's thinking. He was the first to see that scientific knowledge could give men power over nature and believed nature had to be 'hounded in her wanderings', 'bound into service' and made a 'slave'.[8] Bacon wrote: 'the aim of the scientist was to torture nature's secrets from her'[9] – a very cruel mindset and it is worth noting that at this time England was deep into witch trials and, as Attorney-General for James I, Bacon was used to these prosecutions. As nature was perceived as female it is clear that his worldview of 'female' was at play here, where widespread torture of women was rife in the early seventeenth century in England. However, Bacon was to influence the method we know today as science.

Bacon tried to persuade James I to establish a royal institution to advance science and to found a college to study experimental sciences. He also wanted to establish professorships of the new science founded at Oxford and Cambridge. He achieved none of these during his lifetime but when Charles II founded the Royal Society its members used Bacon's scientific approach. Later, both Newton and Darwin acknowledged his contribution. Bacon believed that the only way to advance our knowledge of the natural world was through controlled and systematic procedure.

The first step was to observe the facts, record these observations and amass a body of reliable data. Bacon said this should be done by many people working together rather than by an individual working alone. Then these scientists should identify regularities and patterns which would emerge from the data as causal connections. Finally experiment would confirm the hypothesis and then scientists could say this is a law of nature and accurate predictions could be made. Scientific method was being born. At the same time in France another man was conceiving similar ideas.

A method for absolute certainty

René Descartes was born in France in 1596. As a young man he travelled Europe as a soldier and saw the world as full of contradictions. The religious Reformation had left scepticism around – there were no firm foundations to construct a worldview.

At only 23 years of age, Descartes had the vision to develop a method that would enable him to build a complete science of nature about which there would be absolute certainty. He wrote: 'all science is certain, evident knowledge. We reject all knowledge which is merely probable and judge that only those things should be believed which are perfectly known and about which there can be no doubts'.[10] It was his idea to measure the position of a point by its distance from two fixed lines. Today when we look at a graph we are looking at something invented by Descartes.

A mathematician, he developed a new method of reasoning, which was explained in *Discourse on the method of rightly conducting one's reason and searching the truth in the sciences*. The method is analytic study, where things are broken up and arranged in logical order. It has become the characteristic of science and has resulted in many theories about the world we live in and how we see reality. If you have a problem today, do you try to break it up and tackle it in a logical way? This became the foundation of all future science.

Descartes introduced some fundamental beliefs into Western thinking. He believed scientific discovery started with facts from which logical consequences would transpire through deductive reasoning. He convinced people that this method would make possible a mathematically based science that would give human beings reliable knowledge about the world which was certain.

The universe is a machine

This picture of science became known as the Cartesian worldview and today still has many followers. To Descartes and others the universe is a machine with no purpose or spirituality. Everything works according to mechanical laws and everything can be explained.

A Cartesian worldview that has had a profound effect on Western thought has been the separation between mind and matter or body. This can be seen in Western medicine. Descartes separated the mind – the 'thinking thing' – and matter – the 'extended thing'. Nature was based on mechanical laws and everything could be explained. He, more than Bacon, persuaded Western thinking that certainty was available in our knowledge of the world if we used the right method.

Descartes tried to give a precise account of all natural phenomenon in one single system of mechanical principles but failed. However, his method of reasoning shaped Western thought for three centuries. His only adversary was Spinoza, who disagreed with the notion of two different substances – one of matter, the other of mind. Spinoza argued that whether we describe the universe in terms of our religious conceptions or in terms of planets and other material objects we are in fact describing the same thing. One category is mental, the other material. But they are two different ways of describing the same reality. From this he saw that God was not outside the world, separate; but God was not in the world either. For Spinoza, God was the world.

Rational thought

One of the individuals in rational seventeenth century thinking was Englishman John Locke, who tried the same Cartesian rational approach to society and the behaviour of individuals. He then tried to apply the principles of human nature to economic and political problems. Locke was educated at Westminster School and then Christs Church, Oxford, where he became a don before qualifying as a doctor. It was here that he became involved in both politics and medical research.

Locke saw the human mind at birth as a blank sheet of paper on which knowledge, acquired through sensory experience, is imprinted. This influenced two schools of classical psychology, behaviourism and psychoanalysis, as well as political philosophy. Like Descartes, Locke agreed that there was a distinction between body and mind. He agreed with Descartes that 'I know I am a thinking thing', but he held that 'I don't know my nature, because I don't know what nature a thing has to have in order to be able to think'. For Locke, memory was what mattered to a person and he believed that living awareness of one's own history is what makes the person who they are.

According to Locke, all men were born equal and their development was dependent on their environment. Their actions were always motivated by what they assumed were their own interests. He believed that there were natural laws in society, just as in nature. These included freedom and equality for all and the right to property.

This became the basis of a value system which included free markets, representative government and individualism. It contributed to the thinking of Thomas Jefferson and is reflected in the Declaration of Independence and the American Constitution. Margaret Wheatley sees this thinking in America today. 'In America we raised individualism to its highest expression, each of us protecting our boundaries, asserting our rights, creating a culture that Bellah *et al.* writes "leaves the individual suspended in glorious, but terrifying isolation".'[11]

Locke also influenced the foundations of modern economics. He said that prices were determined objectively, by demand and supply. This enabled merchants to justify high prices and break free from the moral implication of 'just' prices. It also became an economic law as equal as the laws of mechanics and remains today. The mechanistic worldview has influenced much of what we see around us today.

The machine world is complete

The man who completed the mechanistic revolution was Isaac Newton, born in the year of the death of Galileo. By combining Kepler's laws of planetary motion and Galileo's laws of falling bodies (adding gravity), Newton formulated the general laws of motion governing all objects in the solar system – a complete mathematical formulation of the mechanistic view of nature. In so doing, he completed the work of Copernicus, Kepler, Galileo and Descartes.

Newtonian physics from the seventeenth century provided a theory of the world that remained the solid foundation of scientific thought well into the twentieth century. The Church also accepted this and left behind Ptolemy's theory for this world machine, which the Church enjoyed because it implied a great external creator. But very gradually the notion of a divine being disappeared from the worldview, supported by the Cartesian concept of a division between matter and spirit. All that was needed was 'proof' and anything which could be proved, became reality. Zohar describes it as:

> Classical physics transmuted the living cosmos of Greek and medieval times, a cosmos filled with purpose and intelligence and driven by the love of God for the benefit of all humans into a dead, clockwork machine. . . . Human beings and their struggles, the whole of consciousness, and life itself were irrelevant to the workings of the vast universal machine.[12]

Master of nature

It seemed that man indeed was becoming the master of nature and not just in theoretical terms for Newtonian mechanics enabled the development of machinery that made the Industrial Revolution possible. The universe was now seen as one huge mechanical system working according to exact mathematical laws, and nature could be controlled. This worldview was given to the world through Newton's publication

Mathematical Principles of Natural Philosophy (the *Principia*). All physical phenomena are particles held together by gravity.

It is interesting that when we look into the personal background of Newton we find someone with a strong hatred of his stepfather (his natural father having died before Newton's birth), who had deserted his mother, leaving her to struggle and bring her son up alone. Born in Lincolnshire, the son of a yeoman farmer, Newton was a 'late developer' showing no distinction at school or as an undergraduate. But returning home from Cambridge when fear of the plague closed it down, a remarkable career began.

Newton was from this point self-taught and had a strong desire for control in his life so no one could hurt him the way his stepfather had done. This control was extended out into his life's work and an opportunity came to develop his work. His teacher left Cambridge but before going secured the Chair for Newton, giving him, at the age of 27, the freedom to follow his own intellectual inclinations. However, Newton also made volumes of notes on alchemy, apocalyptic texts, unorthodox theological theories and occult matters. He was the last of the 'magicians'.

With a machine scientific worldview it became more difficult to believe in a god which, over time, created a spiritual vacuum. For Newton's universe, like Descartes, had no room for 'purpose'. It was replaced with a rational approach to human issues, which became known as the Age of Enlightenment, and which spread in society during the eighteenth century. The tight control of the Church was losing its grip.

Master of economics

In 1776, Adam Smith published his *Wealth of Nations*. A Scottish philosopher and friend to James Watt, the inventor of the steam engine, Smith was surrounded by machines in large factories and mills. These factories and the new private enterprise influenced his thinking. Smith held that the wealth of a nation would depend on the percentage of people engaged in production resulting from human labour and natural resources. Efficiency and skill would lead to improvements in production with labour saving machinery. Manufacturers also realized that machines could replace workers and used this to keep them insecure and docile. This mindset is still present in the workforce today and was reinforced with downsizing.

Profits were justified as they were needed for more machines. Smith believed that this market system would continue to grow with more and more increase in the demand for goods. He predicted that economic progress would come to an end when the natural limits ran out but that this would be so far in the future it was irrelevant to his theories. The world was an object and machines and men would rule it. It did not matter that we were taking natural resources quicker than they could be replenished. The method of organizing the work was 'management' and it was based on control. If we could control nature, some could control human beings.

More to life than a mechanical world

The German philosopher Kant was in no doubt that Newton and others were right and that to describe the world as an object was essentially correct. However, he also believed that science offered only mechanical explanation, and in areas where such explanations were inadequate, scientific knowledge needed to be supplemented by considering nature as being purposeful. The most important of these areas for Kant was the understanding of life. He believed there was room in this paradigm for concepts such as free will, good, bad and the soul. He concluded that just as the empirical world is governed by scientific laws that are universal, so the moral world is governed by moral laws that are universal. This means that morality is based on reason just as science is based on reason.

Criticizing the notion of a pure, reasoned scientific method was the 'romantic' movement in Germany at the end of the eighteenth century, with people like Herder and Goethe. Goethe saw nature as a living unity, in which mind and matter were inextricably linked. The general idea of the interconnectiveness of nature began – but what of purpose?

Someone who did look at the concept of purpose was Hegel, who was born in Stuttgart in 1770. Hegel had a huge influence on the nineteenth- and twentieth-century world, which is why it is worth exploring his work here.

Evolution of humankind toward absolute knowledge

Hegel saw our concepts as being embedded in ways of life, i.e. our societies. When societies changed, the concepts changed. He saw history and the development of the world as always moving forward. He called this the 'dialectic process' and he believed we would continue to move forward towards the greater development of mind towards freedom. What this means is that history is not a series of accidents, but rather purposeful, moving towards freedom and knowledge. If you had asked him the question: 'Is it individuals or society who are changing?', Hegel would have replied: 'Neither, but what I call *Geist*'. This is where translation becomes difficult. In English *Geist* means 'mind' but it also means the notion of 'spirit'. This suggests a reality beyond the individual mind. Hegel's view is that reality is *Geist*, which is the ultimate essence of being. Our entire historical process is the development of *Geist* towards self-awareness and self-knowledge.

The end point of the dialectical process is Spirit coming to know itself as the ultimate reality and that even those things which seem hostile are part of itself. Hegel calls this 'absolute knowledge'. At this time there is also absolute freedom because now Mind/Spirit is able to order the world in a rational way instead of being controlled by external forces. Once we come to see that we are everything in the world, then we understand the process. For the laws of historical development are in fact the laws of our own reason, our mind and our thinking.

Hegel sees the study of history as a way of getting to know the nature of *Geist*. His greatest work was *The Phenomenology of Spirit*, where he seeks to show that all human intellectual development up to now is the logically necessary working out of Spirit coming to know itself. We are constantly evolving, and changing with us are our notions of religion, the arts, the sciences, ideas, the economy, organizations and society itself. So the music of Mozart could only have happened at the time of Mozart and the idea of capitalism could only happen when it did.

> *Let us bring back poor Sisyphus, who is still pushing his stone up a hill. If Hegel is right, Sisyphus will be changing his understanding of the world, religious beliefs and how society should be governed as he watches the world from his hill-top. Of course people will come and communicate with him and he will ponder over their tales as he pushes the stone. But will hearing the new ideas be enough for Sisyphus to change? Do you have to experience the change or at least be affected by it for the frame of reference to change? Do we have to experience globalization to know it exists? The answer is no, but to change our behaviour to become global, there has to be some internalization which comes from experience. This is how Hegel saw societies changing.*

After Hegel's death his followers split into two movements. The Right were attracted to the rational state and implied that the Prussian state was near to this stage and German nationalism arose. The Left took Hegel's work and said that what was needed was a more far-reaching change, a revolutionary change. His most famous pupil was Karl Marx.

Economic man

Marx took Hegel's evolutionary ideas but replaced one, which was the critical mistake. Marx took the notion that reality is a historical process;

he took the notion of dialectic and that there was an end goal; he took the idea that the end goal was a conflict-free society and until that goal is reached we are condemned to remain in alienation. The great difference is that Hegel saw the process as mental or spiritual. Marx saw it as material and involving control of the economic forces, which if Hegel was right are one of our own concepts anyway. Marx dismissed the notion of *Geist* which was fundamental for Hegel, who believed the only thing that is ultimately real is Spirit, knowing itself as all reality, and each finite spirit is a part of Spirit.

For Hegel, freedom will come when we realize the capacity of human beings collectively to control our own destiny.

This is why, in my view, leadership is so important – but leadership for the collective, not for the few based on position.

The mechanical worldview at the time of Hegel had little or no room, though, for the development of Mind and Spirit. A different paradigm would be needed. What Hegel saw was that in the past, humanity had advanced owing in part to its tendency to reflect on its own condition. In reflecting on a philosophy, we develop new thought or categories that are at most implicit in the philosophy on which we reflect, and in reflecting on historical events we acquire new thoughts that were not available to the participants in those events. We cannot learn from history, since in thinking about our past events we change ourselves, so that our situation and the problems it presents are now importantly different from those of the past.

Did we learn from two world wars? During the past century only one year was without any war going on somewhere in the world. But we ourselves have changed and we react differently today than we did a hundred years ago.

Elsewhere in Europe the idea of evolution was emerging in many aspects of life. The one thing we have seen as we stand in the translatory circle is that there are few ideas that can be ascribed in their entirety to one individual. To begin, evolution had been conceived as a hierarchy – starting with God at the top, then angels, human beings (men first) and animals, and finally lower forms of life.

Another revolution

It was Lamarck who turned the previous hierarchy upside down, saying that we all evolved from simple life. Several decades later, Darwin presented the evidence to support biological evolution in his *Origin of Species*, published in 1859. Darwin's work had the impact of Copernicus. Our view of the world was once again trying to absorb this revolutionary thinking. Copernicus and Galileo had moved the Earth from the centre of the solar system and invoked the wrath of the Church for removing man from the centre of all things. But evolution portrayed by Darwin was far worse for it not only challenged the book of *Genesis*, it also challenged the notion that man was unique for it showed that we evolved from lower forms of life.

Yet evolutionary thinking has forgotten Herbert Spencer, whose ideas on evolution preceded Darwin by at least a decade. Spencer began his working life as a railway engineer but ended as an author. His writings had a deep influence on the way in which society viewed science. He brought science and the concept of evolution into the intellectual world of Victorian Britain and post-civil war America. In 1852 he published an article called 'The development hypothesis' in which he strongly argued the concept of evolution rather than the biblical account of creation.

Spencer also applied his thinking to human history and institutions. His ideas were well received in the UK and Japan, but it was in America that his work received greatest adulation. It was Spencer, not Darwin, who coined the phrase 'survival of the fittest' and the growing class of millionaire entrepreneurs in the USA welcomed this thinking. Today, Spencer is remembered in the UK for his love affair with the writer George Eliot rather than for his work.

However, what Darwin's work gave was 'a place in the world, not as conquerors with spoils but as inheritors with responsibilities'.[13] If we evolved from other life forms then surely we should be much more responsible for all life on this planet.

Science now was an organized institution with its own language and different branches to study different aspects of the material world. It had replaced the Church in influencing how people perceived reality. With it had come the Industrial Age and some men were not only trying to control nature but human life and machines too. If science could separate body and mind and say the world was a machine, what need was there for the human spirit? Like machines, people could work and toil for money to buy products so that more would be needed and more would be bought and so on until here we are today. The Industrial Age influenced writers such as Charles Dickens and William Blake, who wrote:

> Cruelty has a human heart,
> And Jealousy a human face;
> Terror the human form divine,
> And Secrecy the human dress.
> The human dress is forgèd iron,
> The human form a fiery forge,
> The human face a furnace seal'd,
> The human heart its hungery gorge.[14]

Father of new physics

By the end of the nineteenth century evolutionary thinking was spreading and emerged in physics, where physicists such as Max Plank were developing thermodynamics, the science of heat. Through his research, Plank discovered the quantum principle – that energy is emitted not as a continuum but in discrete units, or quanta.

In biology, evolution meant a movement towards increasing order and complexity; in physics because of thermodynamics, it came to mean the opposite – a movement towards increasing disorder. The stage was being set for a paradigm revolution in the twentieth century. The world, we shall see, is not a mechanical machine to be controlled by mankind.

In 1905, two papers were written by Albert Einstein which revolutionized scientific thought. One presented his theory of relativity; the other outlined a new way of looking at electromagnetic radiation which was to become characteristic of quantum theory, the theory of atomic phenomena (atoms and their energy).

A different world

This exploration of the atomic and sub-atomic world brought scientists into contact with a strange and unexpected reality that shattered the foundations of their worldview and forced them to *think* in entirely new ways.

Revolutions like those of Copernicus and Darwin had introduced profound changes in the general conception of the universe, changes that shocked many people, but the new concepts themselves were not difficult to grasp. Now, at the beginning of the twentieth century, physicists faced a serious challenge to their ability to understand the universe and reality.

Every time they asked nature a question in an atomic experiment, nature answered with a paradox, and the more they tried to clarify the situation, the sharper the paradoxes became.

In their struggle to grasp this new reality, scientists became painfully aware that their basic concepts, their language and their whole way of thinking were inadequate to describe atomic phenomena. Their problem was not only intellectual, but involved an intense emotional and existential experience.

One of these scientists was Werner Heisenberg, who remarked: 'I remember discussions with Bohr which went through many hours till very late at night and ended almost in despair; and when at the end of the discussion I went alone for a walk in the neighbouring park I repeated to myself again and again the question: "Can nature possibly be so absurd as it seemed to us in these atomic experiments?".'[15]

Reality itself changes

The working colleagues were Heisenberg, Niels Bohr and Erwin Schrödinger, who found it necessary to change their concepts of space, time, matter, object, cause and effect — in other words, reality itself. Finally, they found a precise mathematical formulation which was to be known as quantum theory or quantum mechanics. It overturned

Newton's work and showed that reality was not static but dynamic, either expanding or reducing.

In these early developments in quantum theory, Einstein deeply re-examined the very basis of Newtonian gravity and finally, in 1915, came up with a revolutionary new theory which provided a totally different picture: his general theory of relativity. Now, gravity was, as Stephen Hawking suggests in *A Brief History of Time*, 'not a force like other forces'.

Einstein wrote in his autobiographical notes:

> Newton, forgive me; you found the only way which, in your age, was just about possible for a man of highest thought – and creative power. The concepts, which you created, are even today still guiding our thinking in physics, although we now know that they will have to be replaced by others farther removed from the sphere of immediate experience, if we aim at a profounder understanding of relationships.[16]

Out of this revolutionary change of reality, this total paradigm shift, a different worldview was emerging which many, though not all, accepted. This reality of the universe is no longer a machine made up of objects, but dynamic, holistic, organic, interrelated and understood as patterns of a cosmic process.

For atoms turned out not to be solid particles but rather vast regions of space in which extremely small particles, electrons, moved around the nucleus. They had a dual nature – sometimes seen as particles, sometimes as waves.

In Newton's physics, the world consisted of tiny, discrete particles – atoms – which bump into, attract or repel each other. They were solid and separate, each occupying its own definite place in space and time. Wave motions were thought of as not fundamental things in them-selves. For quantum physics, however, both waves and particles are equally fundamental. Each is a way that matter can manifest itself, and both together are what matter is. However, we can never focus on both at the same time.

Later it was found that even the sub-atomic particles – the electrons, protons and neutrons in the nucleus – were not solid objects as believed in the old physics. At sub-atomic level, matter does not exist with certainty at definite places, but rather shows 'tendencies to exist' and atomic events do not occur with certainty at definite times and in definite ways, but rather show 'tendencies to occur'. In other words, laws of atomic physics can only be expressed as probabilities. This replaces the Newtonian determinism, where everything about physical reality is fixed, determined and measurable.

A world of interconnections

Our world in the 21st century is not about solid objects we can control. In quantum theory you do not end up with things; you work with interconnections. Particles come into being and are observed only in relationship to something else. They do not exist as independent 'things'. Our world is made up of interconnected energy forces and this is the new paradigm for leadership. Management is about control and is based on the Cartesian mindset of seeing organizations as machines; leadership is about the relationship between a leader and others, and how they interconnect in a web structure bringing about change. Information technology and globalization are both showing the interconnectiveness of our world today. This is why leadership is needed in the world today – the paradigm has changed. Our organizations have to be radically changed not only in structure, but also in thinking.

Heisenberg said: 'The world thus appears as a complicated tissue of events, in which connections of different kinds alternate or overlap or combine and thereby determine the texture of the whole'.[17]

Einstein had difficulty accepting the existence of non-local connections and the resulting nature of probability, which became a debate with Bohr in the 1920s and lead to Einstein's famous remark: 'God does not play dice'. However, in the end Einstein admitted that quantum theory as interpreted by Bohr and Heisenberg formed a consistent system of thought. But he remained of the belief that there was some external reality, consisting of independent, separated elements. Just as Newton had remained in part a 'magician' or alchemist, so Einstein, father of the new physics, remained in part Cartesian. But his contribution was immense in understanding our world and came about through his leadership gifts, which included immense creativity and imagination.

Decades later, John Bull showed that the Cartesian conception of reality as consisting of separate parts joined by local connection is incompatible with quantum theory. There is no separate reality – everything is interconnected. In 1982, Alain Aspect, a French physicist, began a series of annual experiments proving that elementary particles are, indeed, affected by connections that exist unseen across time and space. Finally, in the present time we believe the world is expanding, that there is no centre to the universe and that it probably began with the 'big bang'.

How much reality can science give us?

Science has given us greater understanding of the world but it too is now being scrutinized. People are beginning to question the authenticity of scientists. A recent example is the public disbelief in the scientists advising the government on genetically modified foods. We are also aware of the limitations of science as in Dolly the sheep, which, it turns out, is not a pure clone after all. This also brings into question the ethics of science and its boundaries on ethics and who should decide this. Science itself is now being challenged as a worldview. Science itself may evolve in the new millennium.

Science and leaders

Will science give us the understanding of our world we need to become leaders?

No one can dispute that science has explained a great deal about our world and from this we have created a worldview and mindset. But much of the scientific view of the world is still Newtonian and it is in this paradigm that leadership is at present being taught, which is why this leadership is more management than leadership.

Today the body of science is being questioned about its influence just as the Church was when it controlled the worldview. Even within the scientific community itself there is disharmony. For many, science is about methods and this creed is followed:

> The system called 'empirical science' is intended to represent only one world: the 'real world'. How is the system that represents the real world distinguished? The answer is: by the fact that it has been submitted to tests, and has stood up to tests. Therefore for many, empirical science should be characterized by its *methods*.

Others believe that science is about building knowledge:

> Science is supposed to be about finding out things – *knowledge*. This is true, but in a restricted way. The mere repetition of experiment and observation, the amassing of data and information is not sufficient; scientific activity is guided by ideas, by theories, by the desire to acquire significant information.

> The scientist wishes to make a contribution to public knowledge, and therefore tries to direct his work so that it has relevance to general notions shared by the scientific world. When it was predicted that there should exist a particle with certain properties it was obvious to many scientists that they should look for this particle, and it was not very long before the particle was observed. Indeed, we do not say that a discovery has been made, unless the experimenter was quite unaware of the significance of his result.

> Therefore this definition of science implies that there must be large regions of ignorance, where the writ of public knowledge does not run. Science then is *an organized way of building knowledge*.

Science is a human activity

However, there is another way of looking at science which has emerged in the past century: as a *human activity*. As such, we can say that an individual learns science by being socialized into the shared paradigm of the scientific community with its shared rules of scientific practise. Karl Popper wrote: 'At any moment of time we and our values are products of existing institutions and past traditions. Admittedly this imposes some limitations on our creative freedom and on our powers of rational criticism'.[18] There is no doubt that science is influenced by the thinking of a particular time; however, we can also say that this influence is two way. As scientific progress moves forward it affects not only the scientists' understanding of the world but people beyond this community. So, for example, evolution was explored for a long time before Darwin's publication arrived, and over time the theories of evolution have replaced those in society based on *Genesis*.

Popper's contribution in understanding science is his belief that observation can never prove a theory but can only disprove or falsify it. He did not doubt that scientific theories were true, but he rejected the belief that we can ever *know* that a theory is true. Karl Popper's concern is that the rules of the game of science are dependent on the social and historical location of particular groups of scientists. Since some groups and individuals are seen to be more powerful than others, Popper says we have relativism grounded in power.

One of the best-known writers on science is Thomas Kuhn, who wrote: 'Paradigms change . . . cause scientists to see the world of the research-engagement differently. In so far as their only recourse to that world is through what they see and do, we may want to say that after a (scientific) revolution, scientists are responding to a different world'.[19]

This concept of a paradigm shift was first introduced by Thomas Kuhn in his book *The Structure of Scientific Revolutions*.[20] Kuhn introduced the notion of a scientific paradigm as 'a constellation of achievements – concepts, values, techniques etc. – shared by a scientific community and used by that community to define legitimate problems and solutions'. Changes in paradigms, according to Kuhn, occur in discontinuous, revolutionary breaks called paradigm shifts. We saw this in the Copernicus revolution, the evolution revolution and the quantum revolution.

Most scientists do not question the paradigm. Instead they solve puzzles that extend the scope of the paradigm rather than confront or challenge it. Kuhn called this 'normal science': 'the activity in which most scientists inevitably spend most of their time, is predicated on the assumption that the scientific community knows what the world is like. Much of the success of the enterprise derives from the community's willingness to defend that assumption, if necessary at considerable costs'.[21] Then anomalies accumulate, phenomena that cannot be accounted for, and these eventually trigger a revolution. 'And each transformed the scientific imagination in ways that we shall ultimately need to describe as a transformation of the world within which scientific work was done'.[22]

At the end of his book, Kuhn states that science, like life on earth, does not evolve toward anything, but only away from something. He regards science as a great problem solver which has produced the greatest creativity of human enterprise. Both he and Popper believe that science has only scratched the surface of the truth and do not see it as ever being able to answer all our questions.

Science as an institution

So how has the scientific community survived these revolutions? Talcott Parsons had a theory about social systems (science being one). He claimed that any social system is tied to four 'functional imperatives' which enable it to survive:

1. The system must adapt to environmental changes.
2. It must define the system's goals and manage resources to achieve them.
3. The system must establish control procedures which regulate internal relations within itself.
4. The system must maintain the motivating patterns whereby 'cultural values' are institutionalized.[23]

Therefore science has become an institution, a system, just like many other organizations. Our world in the twentieth century has been created very much by the activity of science. You can see it physically in our cities, our transportation and communication systems. It is also created institutionally in our political and administrative procedures, and in the way we organize our society.

Yet we also realize that scientists are tied to their historical and social locations. This is echoed in Kuhn's statement: 'When Aristotle and Galileo looked at swinging stones, the first saw constrained fall, the second a pendulum'. Kuhn's strongest statement is: 'reality itself is made by the scientist, rather than discovered by him'.[24]

Some argue that while scientists do speak of discovering laws that explain things, it is not the 'laws' or 'theories' that explain, it is physicists who 'explain' physical phenomena, biologists who 'explain' biological phenomena etc., and so scientists who provide scientific explanations of these phenomena. A scientific truth, in this view, is one that is warranted as such by the consensus of a scientific community. Since there are different scientific communities with different standards for warranting the truth, it follows, then, that, truth is *relativized*. This begs the question of whether reality is 'out there', fixed and ultimate, waiting to be discovered, or relative and personal to one's own life experience.

Reality and truth

Mannheim appears to reject the idea that there exist firm, unchanging, ultimate truths. He writes: 'we must reject the notion that there is a sphere of truth in itself, as a disruptive, and unjustifiable hypothesis'.[25] For Wittgenstein and some others, various sciences, disciplines and paradigms must be seen for what they are: artificial, constructed languages that create 'possible' worlds.

For others the scientific methodology is a problem. They argue that firstly the attraction of this 'method' is that it can serve as the basis for further research. Secondly, it is given status and authority by the scientific establishment and relies on consensus by this community. Finally, the methodology is a way of behaving and working – it is a scientific paradigm. The paradigm is never judged or tested – in fact, it itself is the basis for judgement. This can be seen when it has to deal with phenomena such as Uri Geller, where it is up to Geller to prove his credibility to them using their methodology as it, and it alone is the 'finder of truth'. This community even has its own uniform – the white coat, whether in a laboratory or hospital – to give it credibility and status.

For Paul Feyerabend, the human compulsion to find absolute truths, however noble, too often culminates in tyranny. He saw science as having the power to obliterate the diversity of human thought and culture. Feyerabend also rejected the idea that science is superior to other knowledge and criticized the tendency of the West to impose its products of science on others. For Roger Penrose in *The Emperor's New Mind*, all the power of scientific knowledge could not account for the ultimate mystery of existence, human consciousness.

For the realists, which includes most scientists, conceptual truths are about the world and not about language. They hold that language is simply a copy of pre-established structures. For the realists, the key to truth is provided by pure thought, of which logic and mathematics are the clearest examples. Mathematics has been at the core of the unfolding of the physical world and from it we have uncovered more and more constant equations embedded in physical reality. But it has also raised more and more questions.

In addition, there is a belief in the world that with scientific progress comes social progress, and together these will overcome the difficulties in the world today. Is this the case? Are we happier today? Are we free?

Limits of science

The most we can say is that science is an organized attempt to understand reality. However, it has its limits, which were boldly stated by Wittgenstein: 'The whole modern conception of the world is founded on the illusion that the so-called laws of nature are the explanations of natural phenomena'.[26] He added that even when all possible scientific questions had been answered the problems of life would remain completely untouched. It would appear that Xenophanes in Ancient Greece had a point when he wrote:

as for certain truth, no man has known it,
Nor shall he know it, neither of the gods
Nor yet of all the things of which I speak,
For even if by chance he were to utter
The final truth, he would himself not known it:
For all is but a woven web of guesses.[27]

However, we have to say that successful use of science has added to our knowledge of the world. When it is unsuccessful the blame is laid with the incompetence of scientists, equipment or unknown elements causing disturbance rather than its limitations.

'When a hypothesis enters a scientist's mind, he checks it by calculation and experiment, that is by the mimicry and pantomime of truth. Its plausibility affects others, and the hypothesis is accepted as the true explanation for the given phenomenon, until someone finds its faults. I believe the whole of science consists of such exiled or retired ideas; and yet at any one time each of them boasted high rank; now only a name or pension is left'.[28] Yet those scientists also experienced triumph and luck, and a few such as Einstein expressed their imagination.

The lessons from science to this point are two-fold. The first is that the results from scientific work are never absolute, but may be replaced in time by better models having greater descriptive and predictive power – if power over our universe is still the goal. This leads to the second point, which is that scientifically acquired and tested knowledge is not knowledge of reality, it is knowledge of the most persuasive description of reality we have at that moment in time. Yet science has deeply influenced our worldview. It is this worldview that is affecting how we see and run organizations and how we perceive leadership.

Worldviews

For thousands of years, people have been trying to understand their relationship to the rest of the universe. This is fundamental to leadership as a new understanding of the universe is emerging. Today, at the beginning of the twenty-first century, there appear to be three main worldviews.

For most, there is a certain *common picture of ourselves as human beings* which does not fit easily with our overall scientific conception of the physical world. We think of ourselves as conscious, free, mindful, rational beings in a world which science tells us is mindless, without purpose, composed of meaningless physical particles.

This conflict is caused by the second worldview from those in *the scientific community whose paradigm is Cartesian*. They talk about the twenty-first century in the Cartesian seventeenth century vocabulary, in particular, following Descartes' notion of separating mind and body – that it is only material 'things' which are important and our goal is to control them. This can now be reflected in our economic world, our political world, and in the way we structure organizations and our management of those organizations throughout society.

Today there is a third paradigm growing among scientists, philosophers and people which sees the world as *connections*. It was Einstein and his colleagues who showed this to the scientific community with quantum theory. But it also includes another area of knowledge which we have not yet explored. The new paradigm for our world is complete when we add the knowledge also gained in the twentieth century by engineers, physicists, biologists and a handful of others. The field is known as *systems*. When a systemic approach also becomes part of the new paradigm, we can translate leadership into the world in its right context.

The world is a system

One of the pioneers of systems analysis was the RAND Corporation, a military research and development organization founded in the 1940s. During the 1950s systems analysis went beyond military applications, and Stafford Beer developed his ideas in the book *The Brain of the Firm*, first published in 1972. During the 1980s Hans Ulrich at the St Gallen Business School in Switzerland developed a model based on the view of the business organization as a living social system. During the 1990s Peter Senge and his colleague Arie de Geus developed similar ideas.

However, the writer and physicist Fritjof Capra was the biggest influence on me and my work when I read *The Turning Point* in 1982. I had written a seminar paper on 'Science: realism or relativism' and the subject was so alluring to me that afterwards I came across Capra's book. He wrote: 'The systems view looks at the world in terms of relationships and integration. Systems are integrated wholes whose properties cannot be reduced to those of smaller units. Instead of concentrating on basic building blocks or basic substances, the systems approach emphasizes basic principles of organization'.[29]

He goes on to show their dynamic nature. 'Another important aspect of systems is their intrinsically dynamic nature. Their forms are not rigid structures but are flexible yet stable manifestations of underlying processes'.[30] This is the approach we need to take to organizations.

A shock for twentieth-century science was that systems cannot be understood by analysis (Descartes' method). The properties of the parts are not intrinsic properties, but can be understood only within the context of the larger whole. Therefore scientific method is problematic and limiting – it can only show us fixed laws, and life is much more than only fixed laws.

Systems thinking does not concentrate on basic building blocks, as much of science does, but rather on basic principles of organization. Descartes' influence has been to teach Western civilization that when you find complexity you break it up into component parts and tackle each separately. Many management consultants still use this method, which is why their interventions do not achieve the desired results.

Systems thinking, however, questions the Cartesian assumption that a component part is the same when separated as it is when part of the whole. Systems thinking is contextual, which is the opposite of analytical thinking. Analysis means taking something apart in order to understand it; systems thinking means putting it into the context of a larger whole:

> One strives to look at the entire problem as a whole, in context, and to compare alternative choices in the light of their possible outcomes.[31]

Part of the classical theory of evolution is the idea that in the course of evolutionary change and under the pressure of natural selection, organisms will gradually adapt to their environment until they reach a fit that is good enough for survival and reproduction.

In the systems view, evolutionary change is seen as the result of life's inherent tendency to create novelty, which may or may not be accompanied by adaptation to changing environmental conditions. Rather than seeing evolution as the result of random mutations and natural selection, we are beginning to recognize the creative unfolding of life in forms of ever-increasing diversity and complexity as an inherent characteristic of all living systems.

We are all interrelated

Theories such as the Gaia hypothesis, which sees the earth as a living organism actively engaged in creating the conditions that support life, are gaining credibility. Instead of being a machine, the world at large turns out to be unpredictable and sensitive to small fluctuations and certainly not to be controlled by man – though we have the capacity to destroy it.

While it is true that all living organisms are ultimately made of atoms and molecules, they are not nothing but atoms and molecules. There is something else, something non-material, and that is a pattern of organization – networks of interrelationships. This is what I discovered when working with the RAF Red Arrows. Team roles were not the influencing factor – it was the process which evolved from the interrelationships. The model I developed from this was two chains which, when developed together, created a synergy in team performance.

Brain connections

There are other examples around us, one of which has resulted from studying our own brains. It was a fallacy to see the brain as having separate centres for different functions. If we take language, there is no single centre for this in the brain. Instead the brain divides this up. Therefore we have to study how the brain works together and interacts. The brain is made up of neurons which send and receive signals. Electrical impulses trigger the release of a chemical that produces a molecular 'handshake', which in turn results in another electrical signal.

During the birth and first two years of an infant, the brain grows in connections – not in the number of brain cells. It is these connections which separate us from other living creatures. These connections fight for survival in the brain and if we do not use them, they disappear. The connections are greater when there is stimulus, so the more the brain is exercised, the more dense the connections. The mind is the personal brain and the two are connected, not separate.

Anyone who has experienced ME knows that on the days when you cannot walk, move, or lift anything or read, you are also tearful. A doctor will say that it is the mental side of the body affecting the physical – i.e. it is all in the mind. Yet you know the reality is that both mental and physical energy drop like bullets together resulting in the muscles refusing to work all over the body while inside you are feeling pathetic, frustrated and weepy.

Physicist David Bohm wrote: 'The mental and the material are two sides of one overall process that are (like form and content) separated only in thought and not in actuality. Rather there is one energy that is the basis of all reality. . . . There is never any real division between mental and material sides at any stage of the overall process'.[32]

The universe is energy

Scientists say that the whole physical universe is energy, including human beings, as we too are made from atoms. Therefore, the trees, the rocks, animals everywhere, human beings, the products that we make all share the same basic ingredient of energy. When we see this, it also becomes clear that we are all connected in a field of energy and this has repercussions we have all experienced. We know that similar energies attract each other like magnets. Have you noticed that your close friends are very similar to you? Each will be different but reflect a part of you. When you change or go through a personal transformation in your life, you know it is time to let some of those friends go because they are still where you were on your life journey and you have moved on. It is something that occurs to all of us.

In addition, have you noticed how the same idea emerges among people at the same time even in different parts of the world? We can see this in the translatory circle. It seems that when there is a readiness for an idea, it travels and we see synchronistic happenings. Is there something in Hegel's dialectic? Are we moving towards Absolute Knowledge? It is hoped that in this thinking and understanding circle the world has opened for you. You need to understand the world we all live in to express your leadership gifts.

Change the structures

Becoming more aware of our surroundings, translating this under-standing and identifying ourselves as part of a whole interconnected world is part of the new paradigm shift – to understand our world and selves without the constraints of the Cartesian mindset of separating parts and seeing the universe and organizations as a machine. Since the Industrial Revolution we have been control orientated and have developed the principle of material acquisition. Responsibility and power have been centralized on a global scale. Larger and larger hier-archies contain workers where the boss is expected to have the solutions. However, this will change during the next couple of decades.

Margaret Lulic describes the consequences: 'The pattern encourages a victim mentality and a narrow understanding of self-interest. It is repeated in the individual, the family, the community, the school and workplace, because social systems are fractal in nature, just like physical systems'.[33]

We are trying to mend society with separate answers. We break up health, education, social services, the law and economics into large departments in separate buildings. In dealing with poverty we have to resolve the whole of a child's life, not parts, to make it better. If we do not it leaves that young person and many more to become more dependent, either through state benefit or the prison service.

We also try to mend the human body in the same way and for some things it works. However, a great deal of preventive medicine would be more effective if medicine was taught differently. The human body has traditionally been seen as having three separate systems. The *nervous system*, which consists of the brain and network of nerve cells, deals with memory, thought and emotion. The *immune system*, consisting of the spleen, bone marrow, lymph nodes and the immune cells circulating through the body, acts as the body's defence system, controlling wound healing and tissue repair. The *endocrine system* consists of the glands and hormones and is the body's regulatory system, controlling and integrating various bodily functions.

Research in the USA has identified a group of molecules called peptides that act as molecular messengers interconnecting the three systems. So now for some people even within the scientific community of medicine, the body is seen as a single physical and psychosomatic network, not as separate parts. However, there is great resistance to this view from those who still think in the Cartesian mindset, and hospitals are set up with separate departments with doctors for separate parts of the body.

New work

We do the same with organizations, which now need to be rebuilt so that leadership can flourish. Peter Senge has done much work on organizations as systems and learning organizations. He writes: 'Learning organizations demand a new view of leadership. . . . They . . . are responsible for *building organizations* where people continually expand their capabilities to understand complexity, clarify vision, and improve shared mental models . . . there is new work here, and we must be willing to abandon our whole paradigm of who we are as managers to master this new work'.[35]

The constraints to change have come from our old worldview. In the translatory circle you should now begin to see why it was necessary to be here. Until our thinking and worldview change, leadership will remain another management tool. The challenge is for you to take on board the new thinking and worldview which evolves around relationships and connections. Both quantum science and systems thinking have played a part in the new thinking and understanding of the world. Globalization and technology are part of this new paradigm.

The new paradigm for a new millennium

We are slowly coming to understand that we are part of a global community and are learning how to behave as one. As conflicts around the world appear in our living rooms, we are responding on a global scale, as in Kosova and East Timor. For we now realize that both our problems and opportunities have global dimensions. The shift of paradigm requires not only an expansion of our perceptions and ways of thinking, but also of our values and responsibilities.

The old paradigm still sees economics as competitive struggle but through progress and material wealth, through economic and technological growth everything will improve. A paradigm shift is needed here also. Just think what would be possible if politicians and civil servants saw the world as connected and one whole. Today we need to question every single aspect of the old paradigm. We need to challenge the foundations of our modern, scientific, industrial, democratically run, growth orientated, materialistic worldview and way of life. The translatory circle is the questioning and thinking circle.

Having learned who you are and how to be, having explored the world and the realities and thinking we have developed, you are now ready to enter the final circle where you will discover your purpose and a way to express your human gift called leadership.

5

The Transformational Circle

*Never doubt that a small group of thoughtful, committed citizens
can change the world. Indeed it is the only thing that ever has.*
Margaret Mead

The Circular Leadership Journey: The Transformational Circle

*T*he third circle is where individuals apply the lessons of the first two circles to the challenges they face in their world to transform it. This means changing things fundamentally. A useful explanation of what transformation is can be found in the following example.

If you have a jug of water and you change its environment by putting it in the freezer, the water will freeze. It has changed. If you then put it back into its previous environment, it will become water again. When people attend training they often react like the water and turn to ice, but on returning to work, they become water again because the environment has not changed. This is also why change is incremental in organizations when the culture does not change.

Now let us take a stick of wood and set fire to it. This time the wood burns, giving heat until it has changed to ashes, but those ashes can never become wood again because the molecular structure has changed. This is transformation. The water turned to ice and turned back. This is change. The wood transformed to ashes and became something new. This is transformation. In this circle you are going to explore how you can transform some part of the world with your leadership gifts.

Transformational leadership

It was James MacGregor Burns who first used the term 'transformational leadership'. He describes such a phenomenon as:

> Such leadership occurs when one or more persons engage with others in such a way that leaders and followers raise one another to higher levels of motivation and morality. Their purposes, which might have started out as separate but related . . . become fused . . . But transformational leadership ultimately becomes moral in that it raises the level of human conduct and ethical aspiration of both leader and the led, and thus it has a transforming effect on both.[1]

The first fundamental point from James MacGregor Burns is that firstly, leaders *and* followers raise one another to higher levels of motivation and morality. As yet we have not mentioned the concept of followers, which can now be explained. We will all be at different times leaders and followers. We have to stop seeing leaders as being superior and followers as passively doing what they are told to do. As Hughes *et al.* said: 'Leadership is a social influence shared among all members of a group. Leadership is not restricted to the influence exerted by someone in a particular position or role; followers are part of the leadership process too'.[2]

This was expressed in a poem about leadership in the USA:

What does this country need today?
Leadership . . . The country yearns for new leadership for a new
    era.
If led, will the country follow?
But what kind of leadership is the right kind?
The leadership that leads the country in the direction it wants to
    take.
But what specific direction does the country want to take?
Who knows? That's for the leader to figure out. If he is the right
    kind of leader, he will guess correctly . . .
Am I wrong in concluding that it isn't leadership the country
    wants in a President but followership?[3]

The invisible leader

Part of your journey in search of leaders has been to see leadership differently. Included in this is the role we all play at different times as followers. One of the early, and greatest business thinkers was Mary Parker Follett. In a lecture she gave in the 1930s she said: 'Let us not think that we are either leaders or – nothing of much importance . . . Leaders and followers are both following the invisible leader – the common purpose . . . Loyalty to the invisible leader gives us the strongest possible bond of union, establishes a sympathy which is not a sentimental but a dynamic sympathy'.[4]

Therefore, when everyone has the potential to express their leadership gifts we all become leaders and followers. We can, as James MacGregor Burns says, raise ourselves to high levels of motivation and morality to achieve our purpose and transform the world. This is happening today in pressure groups where individuals have achieved more than those inside the political arena. Examples include the Snowdrop Campaign to control firearms and the group that has successfully campaigned to have a memorial for Diana, Princess of Wales. This transforming activity will continue as more and more people express their leadership. This brings us to James MacGregor Burns' second point, which is the transforming effect it has on everyone. How do you do this? He says that during the process leaders' and followers' purposes become fused. So let us clarify the concept of purpose.

Purpose

Purpose is definitely not a title, nor is it about making lots of money. Having a goal of becoming knighted or making millions is just that, a goal, not a purpose. We become our purpose when we make choices to be who we really are.

When we see ourselves and our organizations as machines, we lose what is essentially being human. We go to work, come home, eat and sleep, go to work and so on. We become devoid of will, passion, spirit, compassion and even intelligence. To understand purpose, answer these two questions: what makes you unique and different to everyone else? How can you use this every day through your work? If you are not using this unique gift, you are living removed from your purpose. When you are working with your purpose, work does not feel like a pointless slog.

We will go to another time and place, another story which may help to answer the question.

In the days of misty towers, distressed maidens and stalwart knights, a young man, walking down the road, came upon a labourer fiercely pounding away at a stone with hammer and

> Remember Sisyphus who is condemned to roll a rock to the top of a hill, to see it roll back to the bottom, then to roll it back up the hill to the top, where it again rolls back down, and so on through eternity. What picture do you see from this story? It is probably one where the rock is large and heavy and requires backbreaking work. But work that is hard does not mean it does not have purpose. Important work is seldom easy.
>
> What if Sisyphus' task was to push a pebble up a hill and he had to keep doing this forever? We could even add that each pebble was different and they stayed on top of the hill, making a pile of stones. But there is still no purpose. Why? Is it because there is no point to it? A life without purpose can be simple, repetitive, with no significant result except more of the same. Many live like this, including those with wealth and power. They do the same things day after day, just like Sisyphus. So what is needed to make a life purposeful?

chisel. The lad asked the worker, who looked frustrated and angry, 'What are you doing?' The labourer answered in a pained voice: 'I'm trying to shape this stone and it is backbreaking work'.

The youth continued his journey and soon came upon another man chipping away at a similar stone, who looked neither particularly angry or happy. 'What are you doing?' the young man asked. 'I'm shaping a stone for a building'. The young man went on and before long came to a third worker chipping away at a stone, but this worker was singing happily as he worked. 'What are you doing?' the young man asked. The worker smiled and replied, 'I'm building a cathedral'.[5]

Some believe this is the answer to the question of purpose. Many would argue that what is needed is to give individuals something to enrol in, a vision that is larger than their personal ambitions and careers. This has led to CEOs standing at the front of the workforce explaining the vision for their organization and expecting everyone then to help achieve it. Would this give you purpose in your life?

Creative expression

Let us go back to Sisyphus and the pile of rocks. Suppose these rocks are assembled into something of beauty and grandeur, a mausoleum like the Taj Mahal, which will inspire generations of humankind. To some extent this gives Sisyphus the same motivation as the builder of a cathedral. But he is still subject to the will of others. All his bosses have done is allow him to see what is happening to all the stones he is compelled to move. But he has no role except that of a drone.

Now, suppose Sisyphus not only moves all the stones, but he places them according to a plan which he created using his thought and reason and that the result is an inspiring structure of beauty. Now we see someone with purpose in their life. So now we can answer the question. To have purpose in one's life is a creative expression. This does not come with position, wealth, status or control over others, but adds great value to the world which we all participate in – not as a passive worker, but using ideas and creativity. Having purpose means giving to the world something that would not have existed without that person. It is unique to that person and everyone, rich or poor, has purpose. It is about asking yourself 'what is my personal mission statement?'. It comes from within and transforms the world in either a small or a large way.

The first step, though, begins with you. It was W. Edwards Deming, the quality guru, who said: 'Nothing changes without personal transformation'.[6] Therefore, personal transformation is where we begin. In the first circle the focus was on an inner journey of discovery to find out who you are and what unique gifts you have to offer the world. As you do this you transcend to become all you are capable of. Personal transformation is about taking steps to be different than you were yesterday. From this will come a clear sense of your unique purpose in the world. The problem is that most people are unaware that they have this purpose within them or live their lives always feeling something is missing even if they are rich in material wealth. Instead, they look for meaning elsewhere such as buying expensive new 'toys' or look for excitement in things like extreme sports. But these things never fill the void inside.

Born free

An example of real personal transformation and discovering purpose is expressed in the words of Nelson Mandela:

> I was not born with a hunger to be free. I was born free – free in every way that I could know. Free to run in the fields near my mother's hut, free to swim in the clear stream that ran through my village, free to roast mealies under the stars and ride the broad backs of slow-moving bulls. As long as I obeyed my father and abided by the customs of my tribe, I was not troubled by the laws of man or God.

> It was only when I began to learn that my boyhood freedom was an illusion, when I discovered as a young man that my freedom had already been taken from me, that I began to hunger for it. At first, as a student, I wanted freedom only for myself, the transitory freedoms of being able to stay out at night, read what I pleased and go where I chose. Later, as a young man in Johannesburg, I yearned for the basic and honourable freedoms of achieving my potential, of earning my keep, of marrying and having a family – the freedom not to be obstructed in a lawful life.

But then I slowly saw that not only was I not free, but my brothers and sisters were not free. I saw that it was not just my freedom that was curtailed, but the freedom of everyone who looked like I did. That is when I joined the African National Congress, and that is when the hunger for my own freedom became the greater hunger for the freedom of my people. It was this desire for the freedom of my people to live their lives with dignity and self-respect that animated my life, that transformed a frightened young man into a bold one, that drove a law-abiding attorney to become a criminal, that turned a family-loving husband into a man without a home, that forced a life-loving man to live like a monk . . .

It was during those long and lonely years that my hunger for the freedom of my own people became a hunger for the freedom of all people, white and black. I knew as well as I knew anything that the oppressor must be liberated just as surely as the oppressed. A man who takes away another man's freedom is a prisoner of hatred, he is locked behind the bars of prejudice and narrow-mindedness. I am not truly free if I am taking away someone else's freedom, just as surely as I am not free when my freedom is taken from me. The oppressed and the oppressor alike are robbed of their humanity.

When I walked out of prison, that was my mission, to liberate the oppressed and the oppressor both. Some say that has now been achieved. But I know that that is not the case. The truth is that we are not yet free; we have merely achieved the freedom to be free, the right not to be oppressed. We have not taken the final step of our journey, but the first step on a longer and even more difficult road. For to be free is not merely to cast off one's chains, but to live in a way that respects and enhances the freedom of others. The true test of our devotion to freedom is just beginning.[7]

Purpose is an inner sense of potential and truth. It can involve challenging cultural norms and beliefs. Each individual has a unique purpose, which can range from creating a beautiful garden or helping others learn how to read, to write; to helping a country achieve justice or creating a business that enables people to provide financial security in an ethical way. It is not telling people a vision and expecting them to make it their purpose. It is creating a vision together and having the freedom to express it every day in everything you do.

Make a difference

Margaret Lulic writes: 'There is greatness buried in every soul from the moment of birth . . . to know we make a difference to someone or something beyond ourselves and even beyond our family'.[8]

Does this mean we are all going to go off and pursue our own goals and our families and organizations will suffer? Of course not. Remember what we learned in the second circle – we are all connected. The purpose of one will complement another and we can use our purpose wherever we work. Also ask: are my changes like ice, which will turn back to water, or like ashes, which will remain transformed? Robert Greenleaf said: 'every thing begins with the initiative of the individual'. He wrote: 'The forces for good and evil in the world are propelled by the thoughts, attitudes and actions of individual beings'.[9] In other words, we are not passive hitchhikers in life, but individual beings with purpose. Peter Senge's principle of personal mastery was: 'individuals must have their own visions before a shared vision can exist'.[10]

We need to ask ourselves: what do I really care about? What do I feel passionate about? What does my heart tell me it wants to do? Everyone can find excuses not to follow this need and they really are excuses. Instead ask: who will help me achieve this? When asking someone for help it is an honour for that person, for it enables them to express love and kindness. Most people want to use their purpose for service and fulfilment.

Jobs that are too small

In his book *Working*, Studs Terkel quotes Nora Watson, an editor: 'I think most of us are looking for a calling, not a job. Most of us, like the assembly line worker, have jobs that are too small for our spirit. Jobs are not big enough for people'.[11]

The RAF Red Arrows regard their work to be far more meaningful than just a job. Also, anyone who meets them will quickly realize they are ordinary guys doing extraordinary work. Ordinary people everywhere can do extraordinary things when they find their purpose. Lulic asked the question: 'What do people desire?' To this she answered: 'Feeling meaningful, operating out of integrity, being able to create a comfortable standard of living, free time and making a contribution to something larger than themselves and the workplace'.[12]

The transformational circle reflects the philosophy of Robert Greenleaf, who spent his later life writing about 'servant leadership'. He explains this, saying: 'Becoming a servant leader begins with the natural feeling that one wants to serve, to serve first. Then conscious choice brings one to aspire to lead. That person is sharply different from one who is leader first, perhaps because of the need to assuage an unusual power drive or to acquire material possessions. For such people, it will be a later choice to serve – after leadership is established'.[13] It is clear that our organizations today are run by the latter. To change this, they need to spend time in these three circles and learn. The Dalai Lama said:

> If you seek enlightenment for yourself simply to enhance yourself and your position, you miss the purpose; if you seek enlightenment for yourself to enable you to serve others, you are with purpose.[14]

Where do you start?

We all have a purpose or a mission or a dream. Look deep inside yourself to find yours. When you have found it, where do you start? Adam Michnik was one of the architects of Poland's Solidarity movement where workers fought for freedom in their society under Communism. He said: 'start doing things you think should be done, and start being what you think society should become. Do you believe in free speech? Then speak freely. Do you love the truth? Then tell it. Do you believe in an open society? Then act in the open. Do you believe in a decent and humane society? Then behave decently and humanely'.[15]

When you are clear about your purpose you have meaning, direction and energy to your leadership. You will find others who also have a similar purpose. However, there are two concepts you need to learn to bring about transformation in the world. We begin with a poem:

> purpose is about developing relationships
> purpose is about bringing attention and intention
> into the present moment
> moving ahead with new ideas
> giving and receiving support
> volunteering
> mentoring
> listening to the imagination and intuition
> communicating
> taking action based on inner direction and
> hints from the external
> being adaptable
> taking responsibility and ending the victim stance forever
> surrendering to the divine will and working with the lessons
> developing fluidity, tolerance, compassion, and
> the ability to love.[16]

There are two words in this poem which many discuss in their work and which help us in trying to fulfil our purpose – *attention* and *intention* in the second line. Deepak Chopra writes: 'Attention energizes, and intention transforms'.[17] He explains that when you give something your attention it grows in your life and if you take attention away, it withers away. Gary Zukav explains that every experience reflects an intention. He says that intention is much more than desire because it involves your will. So if you want to change some part of your life, desire alone will not achieve it. But if you truly desire the change it has to begin with the intention to change it.

Organizational renewal

John Gardner in *Self Renewal* (1981) said that leaders should pay attention to both self-renewal and organizational renewal. Roger Harrison suggests the way to achieve this is through 'alignment' and 'attunement'.

Alignment, he says, is when people in an organization act as part of an integrated whole, each finding the opportunity to express his or her own purpose through the organizational purpose. Clearly, this requires everyone to know both their own and the organization's purpose. He sees the organizational purpose as something that should be discovered by its people rather than decided. This involves an internal search for values and meaning. In other words, all employees should be asking: Why does this organization exist? What is it about? What is important to the people who work here? What does it need to survive? Who do we work with outside the organization? What do we need from them? What can we do to ensure this? How are we different from the competition? By doing this, the organization is discovering its place, position and purpose in the larger system.

Attunement, according to Harrison, means developing harmony among the different parts of the system and between the parts and the whole through understanding, caring, mutual support and so on. In this way, human energy is not one-way from individuals to the organization, but the whole also nourishes the uniqueness of each individual. Therefore, there is no conflict between an individual purpose and the organization's purpose. In fact, the purpose will give the organization's vision energy and unify all employees.

A true story

A true story to put this into context is one which tells how a new marketing director suddenly found himself managing director of a computer company that was really having difficult times. Many of the staff had been laid off and the previous managing director had left. The new managing director began by spending time with all the people. This included inviting several to join him for lunch on a weekly basis until he had listened to all of them.

While this was going on he was listening to managers and his top team, who together developed a plan for 100 days to turn the company around. He allowed the managers to develop their plans and together the team had direction, purpose, a set of values that had come from the discussions with staff, and the motivation to make it a reality. He then took every employee away for two days and hired someone to look after the phone calls for this period. The two days involved presenting the plans, responding to feedback, having some team games and finishing with a dinner and the final vision from the managing director, having listened to everyone and taken on board their views.

They returned to work and put into practice the plans. Anyone who did not behave according to the values set out was confronted by colleagues. If a team or department was not helpful, others would find out why and work to resolve things. Within weeks the company turned around and had to start recruiting again. The growth has continued to this day and the buzz can be felt as soon as you walk in the building. People are fulfilling their purpose every day.

It is as Briskin describes: 'We are transformed not by caring for our own soul [spirit] in isolation but by entering into a dialogue with something outside ourselves. It may, at times, be work we care about, or someone we care about, or something we feel needs attention. But whatever, we must know it as something animated by its own powers – a spark of soul [spirit] addressing us'.[18]

Organizational dynamic urge

In the first, transcendent, circle we explored the notion of a dynamic urge. According to Robert Fritz, organizations have a form of dynamic urge which exists in their purpose. It is the energy, drive and spirit you sometimes feel as you walk around an organization. Fritz says that this dynamic urge cannot be constructed artificially. When people understand this drive, the organization can move forward in the right direction. Sometimes it is difficult to put aspects of the purpose into words because it is not verbal, but you can feel it, which is why when managers cause the organization to act in ways that are inconsistent with its purpose, frustration is felt.

The process of transformation is about finding meaning for the organizaton and responding to its generative essence. As long as we see organizations as machines to be controlled, dealing with change will always be problematic. Calling in consultants who also have this perception will also result in disappointment. Instead, if we see the organization as generative, as unfolding in its future through its purpose, transformation becomes real. What is fundamental is to establish the purpose that unifies everyone.

> In the lives of many people it is possible to find a unifying purpose that justifies the things they do day in, day out – a goal that like a magnetic field attracts their psychic energy, a goal upon which all lesser goals depends . . . Without such a purpose, even the best-ordered consciousness lacks meaning.[19]

Organizations are coming to a point of being ready for transformation, but they are prevented by a dying worldview or paradigm and all the thinking and values associated with it. They are also still structured in a hierarchy with the belief that those at the top should decide the purpose.

Be a transformer

The required changes in the thinking and consciousness of individuals cannot be forced but they can be influenced. Before stepping out of this circle you should realize that you are a transformer. The tools you use will be discussion and dialogue. These should be more than discussions about the day-to-day work but include the hopes and fears of yourself and others for the work, for the organization and for all those with whom you interconnect in a world you are a part of, not separate from. You have a crucial role to play. In transforming your life and some part of the world you must spend time in these three circles to learn how to express the fullness and wholeness of your leadership potential. For the challenge will be great.

The reality today is that companies tend to have the same purpose – to make money for shareholders. However, many will have a vision that relates to customers and being the best. The problem is that people's behaviour is not aligned because the actions they see relate to the bottom line, such as further downsizing, which is now called restructuring. Those who are running organizations are stuck in that paradigm of a deeply held, unconscious set of assumptions and values. It is reflected in their behaviour and language of 'bottom line' and 'market forces'. Fundamental to this paradigm are power, position and control. In the public sector, politicians may talk a new language and genuinely desire an equal world, but some of the civil servants who carry out the day-to-day work are still in the old paradigm and will protect their power base.

However, a few individuals are now starting to rethink purpose in more fundamental ways and to realize they have a bigger purpose, which includes serving people, the community and even the world. It is their *actions* which will tell you how much they believe this – such as whether they still have a special parking space and whether they join staff for lunch.

Words are not enough

A factory producing parts for computers, but the parts are faulty, is not attending to its purpose. A hospital that measures its success by waiting lists or revenue but does nothing to enhance the health of its members is not attending to its purpose within the community. A school system which has high grade results but is unable to resolve the numbers of those leaving who cannot read is not working to its purpose. No amount of words in mission statements and visions will resolve this. It can be done only through dialogue about the nature of the work, its connections to the individuals' own purpose and to the outcomes of the organization.

Ask your organization three questions:

1. What is our system (healthcare, education, business) for?
2. What outcomes are required?
3. What is my role in it? Keep expanding your answer.

As Jaworski wrote: 'we all participate in creating the future, not by imposing our will, but by deepening our collective understanding of what wants to emerge in the world, and then having the courage to do what is required'.[20]

A handful of organizations are beginning to realize that when they encourage both personal and organizational purposes to become aligned, when everyone expresses themselves fully, there is a powerful dynamic urge which has far more impact on bottom line than further restructuring. Real transformation can begin.

Enter into dialogue

Individuals have to start thinking and seeing the world differently and you can help – not by shouting about leadership as being part of humankind, but by behaving the part. Talk quietly to people, enter into dialogue, set up a 'new thinking' group in your organization to discuss some of these issues, and behave as a leader. Become what you are capable of, with purpose and heart, and begin transforming your world. Be the leader you are capable of being.

Commit oneself

Goethe said: 'that moment one definitely commits oneself, then providence moves too. All sorts of things occur to help one that would never otherwise have occurred . . . all manner of unforeseen incidents and meetings and material assistance, which no man could have dreamed would have come his way. Whatever you can do, or dream you can, begin it. Boldness has genius, power and magic in it. Begin it now'.[21]

In the transformational circle you can decide what small steps you can take to transform your world. It is here you may decide that the work you are doing at present is not your purpose. Do not be afraid of this. When you start to live your true purpose, it no longer feels like a struggle. Ralph Blum wrote:

> In each life there comes at least one moment which, if recognized and seized, transforms the course of that life forever. Rely therefore, on radical trust, even though the moment may call for you to leap, empty-handed, into the void.[22]

One cold November morning I heard the team manager of the RAF Red Arrows speak at a business breakfast. I felt there was something in what he said that could help other organizations. At the end of the talk I thrust my card into his hand and said: 'Ring me, I've an idea'. A month later I was planning a video and carrying out research. It transformed my work and raised the profile of the Red Arrows into business organizations worldwide.

Desperate for transformation

Before leaving this circle I would like to bring to your attention three areas in human life that are desperate for transformation.

The environment

The first is the way we are treating our own planet. In September 1999 the United Nations launched a report[23] from Dr Klaus Topfer, the world's most senior environmental official. His department has access to the scientific expertise of all parts of the UN. He warned that we are destroying the environment quicker than repairing. He says that progress has been made through the ceasing of chlorofluorocarbons (CFCs), which damaged the ozone layer, cutting back pollutant gases such as sulphur dioxide, which causes acid rain, and on the amount of sewage dumped in rivers, and the way we are teaching children to be environmentally aware. However, he said these gains are being outpaced by the environmental impacts of population and economic growth.

According to Dr Topfer, the two major causes of environmental degradation were the continued poverty of the majority of the planet's inhabitants and excessive consumption by the well-off minority. He says that by 2025 two-thirds of the world's population will have difficulty accessing water. Already 20% of the world population lacks access to safe drinking water and half the world lacks access to safe sanitation. A new global problem is nitrogen. Having been used in fertilizers, it has prompted an explosive growth of toxic algae reaching our seas and has made some fresh water supplies unfit for drinking.

Dr Topfer concludes that there are four areas that need attention. The first is addressing the gaps in our environmental knowledge; second, root causes such as over-consumption have to be tackled; third, environmental thinking needs to be integrated into mainstream thinking and decision making; and lastly, all those affected by environmental problems should be mobilized together. Thus, there is a desperate need for leadership in the whole context of changing the way we are treating our planet.

Education and equality

The second area is education and equality. Recent research in the UK from the National Institute of Economic and Social Research[24] showed that spending on education helps reduce income inequality. During the 1980s and the beginning of the 1990s inequality in the UK increased, with the top tenth of the income distribution getting 26% of the pie. There is now evidence that this dispersion has stopped declining. Therefore, by putting funding into education, earnings across society improve and inequality declines.

If we took this to a global scale the effects would improve the lives of many more. As yet there is no international commitment to education on a global scale. At least once every decade since the Second World War a commitment is made to universal primary education for all children in the world but it has never materialized. This needs to change as the transformation which would follow if such a commitment was made would improve the lives of millions. There is a need for leadership here to enable this to happen.

Human life

The third area is one which had a short inspiration during the life of Diana, Princess of Wales. In March 1999 the Ottawa treaty banning anti-personnel mines came into force. Many of the countries that signed up have destroyed their stocks of the weapons. But in Angola mines are being laid again with even more intensity – and the government signed the treaty. Those that did not sign were notably Russia, China, India and the USA. But 135 countries did sign and the treaty has been ratified by 84 countries, including every member of the EU except Finland.

The USA has said that it will sign by 2006 on condition a replacement can be found for anti-personnel mines, which, it argues have an important military function. Their function at present is killing and maiming. In Angola of the population of nine million people, one in four hundred has mine-related injuries. Leadership is needed here to resolve the high number of people killed and injured every day by mines. To show how these global issues are linked a positive step might be to use the money spent on these weapons on educating every child or ensuring clean water for all.

Small things with great love

Your leadership gifts are needed everywhere in small ways. This includes your communities as well as the world at large. Mother Teresa said:

'Small things with great love. It is not how much we do, but how much love we put into the doing. It is not how much we give, but how much love we put into the giving'.[25] In the transformational circle decide how you can best use your leadership gifts to transform the world in a small way. Remember that to transform is more than change; it means that things will never be the same as they are now. Use your leadership to make a difference.

It is as George Bernard Shaw wrote: 'This is the true joy in life, the being used for a purpose recognized by yourself as a mighty one'.[26]

Finally, it is hoped that you are leaving this third circle a different person than when you began reading this book. You should know more about yourself, the world and how to change it. My final comment is that you are not alone. Everywhere are individuals longing to find their leadership and express it in the world – people like the two in the financial company who spoke to me of their missing part which was inside them. Now you can begin transforming the world and express your leadership with others. Use it wisely.

Kouzes and Posner express what this circle is about: 'As you work to become all you can be, you can start to let go of your petty self interests. As you give back some of what you have been given, you can reconstruct your communities. As you serve the values of freedom, justice equality, caring and dignity, you can constantly renew the foundations of democracy. As each of us takes individual responsibility for creating the world of our dreams, we can all participate in leading'.[27]

6

The Search Continues

Where man is in the world, of the world, in matter, of matter, he is
not a stranger, but a friend, a member of the family, and an equal.
Michel Serres

The journey through this book may be ending here, but the journey to become a leader is not over. When you go back into your
organization you are in danger of returning to doing, doing, doing again
and becoming frustrated because in your heart you know there is a better
way. The danger you have before you now is whether you will be like
water, which turns to ice and then returns to water when back in
the previous environment. Real transformation begins from within you
and the realization that you now know your true authentic self and the
leader you are capable of becoming. This will not be easy as organizations are not yet structured and run in a way for leaders to express
their gifts.

Percy Barnevik, former chairman of ABB and one of the most
respected individuals in the business world, has often said that organizations today allow people to use only 5–10% of their abilities at work,
including leadership. This has been supported by research carried out
on both sides of the Atlantic and is why *In Search of Leaders* is one of

two books. The second book will outline what organizations need to do to enable everyone to practise their leadership. However, do not use the limits of your organization as an excuse not to express your leadership from today.

In Chapter 1 I spoke metaphorically of lights you see just before you go through a black hole in space. The lights I spoke of were global-ization, information technology and knowledge workers. Before you finish this journey here it will help to explore these lights in more detail for they will help you when you return to work. These three beacons of light will guide you as you continue your leadership journey through the world at large. These lights will force change and you can be a pioneer of this change.

Globalization

The first light is the globalization of the world. There is a tendency to see globalization as an economic phenomenon. For a long time trade has crossed national boundaries but the extent to which this occurs is far greater today. The greatest factor is the level of finance and capital. In fact, over a trillion dollars every day is moved around on global currency markets. As Peter Townsend said: 'The world is a web of interconnected trades, organizations, labour markets and professions, not a division into one hundred and eighty autonomous and separate nations'.[1]

Globalization is not just economic. Communications transmit all over the world via over 200 satellites above the Earth. Images from around the world are picked up every day in our homes as we watch world events evolve in our sitting rooms. Technology is global, as with the internet; culture is global as Western films are watched in third-world countries, where the young have aspirations similar to those elsewhere; and political issues are global such as the environment, which is discussed but as yet needs more action. The global world at present has winners and losers.

Act globally

The UN 1997 Human Development Report[2] showed the increase in the polarization between the rich and poor. In fact this doubled between 1981 and 1996. The largest 100 companies have annual revenues that exceed the GDP of 50% of the world's nation states. Five companies in the UK receive almost 50% of everything the British spend. Ten corporations control almost every aspect of the worldwide food chain. And 160 million children are undernourished in the world. The biggest winners have been the multinational corporations.

David Korten writes: 'We are creating a world that is becoming more deeply divided between the privileged and the dispossessed, between those who have the power to place themselves beyond the prevailing market forces and those who have become sacrificial offerings on the alter of global competition'.[3]

What is clear is that economics and politics have to behave and *act* more on a global scale. Governments need to respond to global realities with urgency. Globalization is far more than an economic market. It will affect every aspect of our lives and how we choose to live today. It includes environmental issues, poverty, education, health, the family and work. No longer can we just sing 'One world' – we have to live and be one world. To really understand and realize that we are all interwoven and interconnected requires a paradigm shift, a revolution in how we see ourselves and every other living form. We need a shared, creative response to the issues affecting this planet. Fundamental to this will be leadership throughout for it will be individuals who will bring this about.

These individuals will see that the world we live in is interwoven and interconnected. As such, isolation, whether economic or human, belongs to a past world. What is needed are individuals who have the courage to let go of the old thinking and take themselves to places they have not been to before. Remember the American films of pioneers taking their wagons across open ground into the west for the first time. To progress into a different world, we must find the energy and courage to take the first steps, like the pioneers. New ideas are not usually welcoming and the two areas being attacked are 'power' and 'control'. Resistance will be strong. What can you as an individual do? What could be your first steps in an organization?

Get together with colleagues and establish your purpose in the organization. Be careful that this does not turn into a job description. Your purpose should be a way to identify and put into words why your roles exist and what gives meaning to them. Add to this the behaviours and values you want to attain. Agree that if anyone then acts out of character, the group will challenge them. Be a leader in your organization and others will model their behaviour on you. Leaders teach others to be leaders; you begin by being the pebble thrown into the pond from which ripples reach the whole pond. You will *see* that the world is interconnected and that your actions count.

When the group is comfortable, introduce new ideas. For eventually, individuals will see themselves, others, the organization and the world fundamentally differently. When they see the world differently, thinking and behaviour will change. Globalization will become one world.

Information technology

This second light is technology, which is often perceived to mean computers. In fact, IT is more to do with relationships. The reason why IT does not always achieve its potential is that it is put into hierarchies with managers who see information as inputs and outputs. The result of this has been to create just more information, which is causing more anxiety as managers try to deal with the overload.

A radical way forward is to realize that information should be used to decide the structure. Therefore, new information should allow for new structures. Organizations that have a more flexible structure such as teams moving around are better at using the potential of IT. At the heart are relationships that interact with the information.

In a hierarchy, information flows up and down. Some hierarchies have put into place cross-functional teams to encourage information to flow across. However, the reality falls short as managers jostle for position. Our old structures do not work because control is at the heart of them, in thinking, behaviour and reward. A total paradigm is required before we can really tap into the potential of IT.

It will require leaders who understand IT and use this knowledge not as expertise power for themselves, but to enhance the lives of all at work. IT is for everyone throughout the organization and evolves around relationships with colleagues, with customers and others. Today, an individual can communicate with anyone on the planet, thus showing how interconnected we are becoming.

Circular structures

For organizations, when the structure is circular, information can go anywhere and a more open network operates. We cannot wait for the top of the pyramid to change. Where you work, change the structure to a circle. Encourage others to express their leadership in this environment. Show them the way, for individuals so used to the hierarchy, will tend to shun responsibility, blame the 'system' or other people and give only 10% or less of their potential. Use technology to improve the relationships in the organization and you will begin to create an environment where leadership can be practised.

Knowledge workers

The third light bringing radical change is the recognition of the brains of employees. This is not just about a more highly educated workforce. People serving in shops and on factory floors should be included here as they have expert knowledge on customers and products. Human capital is a source of innovation and transformation based on information flow. It is now clear that what we make, buy, sell and do comes from the basis of knowledge.

A university may have some brilliant people working in it, but it is not intelligent as a whole because there is little flow of knowledge, whereas a company making widgets can be a very intelligent organization if knowledge flows throughout and is even standardized with suppliers and distributors to match market requirements. Why does this not happen everywhere? To date, managers have not been willing, or sometimes able, to create the environment and encouragement to bring out this knowledge, which is in the heads of people. The fault lies with managers, not employees.

At the same time, managers are devolving tasks but not responsibility. It is one thing to tell someone that they are now in charge – but to then add that you would like to be kept informed on a weekly basis is another thing. The message people hear is 'You don't trust me'. So people do what is asked of them and no more. They end up conforming. It is as Peter Wickens says: '[Managers] are not *transformers*, they are *conformers*'.[4]

How much does your organization spend on R&D? If it is less than capital investment you are a producer. If R&D spending exceeds capital investment knowledge, thinking and transforming are at its core.

Organizational structure is fundamental. Thomas Stewart, who has studied knowledge workers, writes: 'Where once there were pyramids, bosses, departments, troops, now there are webs, nodes, clusters, flocks. In companies whose wealth is intellectual capital, networks rather than hierarchies, are the right organizational design'.[5] The circular network organization will triumph over the heavy hierarchies. Will the large hierarchies still be with us in a hundred years? My personal view is they will not.

Building communities

When structure changes, organizations can become communities and everyone can use their leadership potential. MacGregor Burns writes about President Woodrow Wilson calling for leaders who 'could lift people out of their everyday selves'.[6] But people can do this themselves when they have an environment that is a community rather than a patriarchal hierarchy. It is as Warren Bennis said recently: 'The key to future competitive advantage will be the organization's capacity to create the social architecture capable of generating intellectual capital. And leadership is the key to realizing the full potential of intellectual capital'.[7]

The problem for many is that intellectual capital and knowledge cannot be dealt with by accountants, who have a huge interest in organizations. Did you know that accounting as we know it today is around 500 years old? The balance sheet came about in 1868 and the income statement dates from the 1930s. The whole process is for an industrialized world, not a global, intelligent world. Today, a product's costs tend to come from R&D, service and intellectual assets. In fact, all our management systems will change during the next century for they are outmoded. Electronic networks may even lead to questioning of the need for managers themselves. All managers will have to evaluate their relationships with others and how they work. The future will challenge everyone.

Heart of human beings

In a knowledge economy the real value of the organization is the thinking of people, how they process information and develop creative solutions to complex problems which they own. But people cannot think creatively if they are stressed or feeling undervalued. Without trust, freedom and confidence, thinking and knowledge creation does not happen.

What is also missing from the notion of knowledge workers is that people do not just have brains – they also have hearts and energy and spirit. We mentioned the concept of 'persona' in the transcendent circle, but now I would like to explain further the concept as perceived by psychologist William Stern, who, unlike most of his colleagues, tried to develop a systemic and whole approach to human behaviour.

Stern believed that every human being had an essence, which he called the persona. This persona was the body and spirit together and was unique to livings things. This persona is teleological, goal orientated and has a strong urge to live and realize its potential. In addition, the persona is aware of itself and can be part of a larger structure such as a team or an organization. The persona has a relationship with the outside world from birth until it passes away. Fundamental to this idea is that Stern believed a living thing is not passive and could choose how to act or behave.

No limits

To understand ourselves and others means to understand both our internal drives and the forces from the outside environment together. This is why you cannot predict what individuals will or will not do. But with the right environment, human beings could fulfil dreams, be innovative, creative and passionate. We could become the leaders we are all capable of.

Ben Okri reinforced this when he wrote:

> Accept no limitations to our human potential.
> We have the power of solar systems
> In our minds . . .
> Our desire to survive is awesome.
> Our quest for freedom is noble, and great.[8]

US author Gary Zukav[9] sees the human race extending our five senses as we evolve. His ideas also show the manager and the leader coming from their two paradigms. Zukav sees the five-senses human being as alone in a physical universe trying to control and dominate it to survive, whereas Zukav's multi-sensory human being is never alone in a universe which is intelligent, conscious and alive. In this world life is a garden for learning created by all the individuals who share it. Everything that happens in this world is for us to experience and learn from.

Make the future

Many organizations today are still five-sensory entities while human beings within them desire to be multi-sensory. Knowledge workers also desire to be heart workers with purpose and meaning. Treat individuals in your organization as whole individuals with leadership gifts and you might, just might, start a ripple effect and become the leader you too are capable of becoming.

Have the courage to be different; be yourself, brains and heart. Be a leader and live these words from Ben Okri every day:

> We that are here now are touched
> In some mysterious way
> With the ability to change
> And make the future.
> Those who wake to the wonder
> Of this magic moment
> Who wake to the possibilities
> Of this charged conjunction,
> Are the chosen ones who have chosen
> To act, to free the future, to open it up,
> To consign prejudices to the past,
> To open up the magic casement
> Of the human spirit
> Onto a more shining world.[10]

A new organization to support you

In 1999 a new organization was formed called the Institute of Leadership. It is a non-profit organization whose focus is to offer unbiased and up-to-date research, information and support on leadership. Its purpose is:

> To further the understanding of leadership in the world and facilitate the development of leadership potential throughout society.

The Institute is connected globally through the internet and at its core is an information gateway to all the information around on leadership.

At the Institute, we work with individuals, universities and schools, organizations and training providers to influence how to develop leadership potential in society. To enhance this, The Leadership

Challenge has just been launched. Here, a hundred individuals from all walks of life will have a unique opportunity to develop their potential in some innovative ways over a twelve-month period. Our aim is to offer this process to as many people as possible every year. The Institute will offer individual and corporate membership.

Developing young people

However, a bigger role is to influence schools to change the way they develop young people. Education is far more than storing facts. It also has to stop being a choice between subject areas such as either science or arts, putting young people into boxes or failing many who leave with not much of a future. Mary Parker Follett was an inspiration to many writing on leadership; she also spoke of education:

> So in the education of our young people it is not enough to teach them their 'duty'; somehow there must be created for them to live in a world of high purpose to which their own psychic energies will instinctively respond. The craving for self-expression, self-realization, must see quite naturally for its field of operation the community. This is the secret of education: when the waters of our life are part of the sea of human endeavour, duty will be a difficult word for our young people to understand; it is a glorious consciousness we want, not a painstaking conscience. It is ourselves soaked with the highest, not a Puritanical straining to fulfil an external obligation, which will redeem the world.[11]

Today we are boxed and labelled success or failure by the time we reach our teens. Creativity, innovation and leadership are suppressed. These limitations stay with us for life. Leadership is perceived as the position of 'top dog' and so the majority of young people do not perceive themselves as leaders who can influence and change the world. This has to change. At the same time, while schools exercise the analytical, IQ left side of the brain they tend to neglect the intuitive, EQ right side. So we are growing half human beings with half their capability. Today, the world needs whole individuals who can express their leadership. For our future as human beings will depend on it.

Our schools and universities are today designed and run for a past world. There is a huge challenge for education, which goes beyond training the head or principal to be 'General'. Places of learning must become learning organizations and freed up from huge process constraints and power politics.

Learning is synonymous with leadership. The aim of standing in the three circles is to stop doing and rushing around and instead take a journey to become the leader you are capable of becoming. Alvin Toffler wrote: 'The illiterate of the future will be those who do not know how to learn'.[12]

Albert Einstein was once asked by a mother what she should do to encourage her child to be intelligent like him. Einstein answered her by saying that she must read fairy stories to the child. To this the mother then asked what she should do after that. Einstein said she should read more fairy stories. For Einstein knew imagination was key to a creative and intelligent mind. Imagination obliterates constraints in our thinking. It will be paramount for our future.

Leadership

Leadership is one of the most difficult concepts to understand. As such, it has been perceived as something 'mystical' and rare. The question many researchers, journalists and writers are asking at present is: where are our leaders? The answer is: everywhere. Begin by looking into a mirror and then look at all the leaders around you. Charles Handy sums up the message at the end of this journey here:

> We should trust ourselves to be both great and good, and if sometimes that trust is misplaced, more often it will be merited, for there is that within all of us which cries out for a better and a fairer world.[13]

The bottom line here is that it will be individual leaders expressing their potential and gifts which will change the world. Carl Jung wrote:

> In the last analysis, the essential thing is the life of the individual. This alone makes history, here alone do the great transformations just take place, and the whole future, the whole history of the world, ultimately spring as a gigantic summation from these hidden sources in individuals. In our most private and most sub-jective lives we are not only the passive witnesses of our age, and its sufferers, but also its makers. We make our own epoch.[14]

The search for leaders is a search for the human spirit and it is everywhere. No more must we sit back and wait for someone to change things and make the world better. We each have a role to play. If you use every day and every experience to learn, you will know how to express your leadership gifts. The journey now really begins.

The Institute of Leadership

The purpose of the Institute of Leadership is to further the understanding of leadership in the world, and facilitate the development of leadership potential throughout society. Our mission is to provide the best information, expertise and support in the field of leadership. We will achieve this through:

- A Centre of Knowledge based on research and an information gateway via the internet.
- Projects which will take us into the wider community.
- A Leadership Forum for ideas, learning and support for members.
- A process of development for organizations to enable individuals to practise their leadership potential.

The seven essences of leadership explained here are at the heart of the Institute. In addition all activities carry with them the values of integrity, purpose, personal effectiveness, understanding of the world and responsibility.

Institute of Leadership
Telephone: 01242 262640
Visit our web site at: www.IofL.org
or email me at: hilarie.owen@IofL.org

References

Preface

1. John Kotter, The leadership factor, *Harvard Business Review*, 1988
2. Ashridge Research Group, *Management for the Future*, Ashridge Management Centre, England, 1988
3. Marione Devine, Big chiefs fail the leadership test, *Sunday Times*, 17 July 1988
4. Chris Woodhead, report for the Dept of Education and Employment, February 1999
5. Centre for Research in Employment and Technology in Europe, Leadership Report, 1996
6. Industrial Society, Liberating leadership, Industrial Society, London, 1997
7. Conversation with Nigel Nicholson from the London Business School
8. Watson Wyatt Consultants, USA, 1999
9. James MacGregor Burns, *Leadership*, Harper & Row, New York, 1978

Introduction

1. Michael Simmons, *New Leadership for Women and Men*, Gower, 1996.
2. What's happened to leadership? *Time Magazine*, 1993 (quoted by Paul Taffinder in *The New Leaders*, Kogan Page, London, 1995)
3. Simon Heffer, 'Why we don't produce great leaders?', *Daily Mail*, 1998
4. John W. Gardner, The cry for leadership, in *The Leader's Companion*, ed. J. Thomas Wren, Simon & Schuster, New York, 1995
5. Robert Greenleaf, *Servant Leadership*, Paulist Press, 1977

Chapter 1

1. Anthony De Mello, Song of the bird (quoted by Anthony De Mello, in *Awareness*, HarperCollins, London, 1990)
2. Diane Fassel, *Working Ourselves to Death*, HarperCollins, London, 1990
3. *Fortune Magazine*, 1994
4. A.R. Ammons, *Tape for the Turn of the Year*, W.W. Norton, New York, 1965
5. Alan Briskin, *The Stirring of the Soul in the Workplace*, Berrett-Koehler, San Francisco, CA, 1998
6. Alan Briskin, op. cit.
7. European Foundation for the Improvement of Living and Working Conditions, *New Forms of Work Organisation*, Dublin
8. Warwick University, UK; research carried out by Professor Andrew Oswald and Professor David Blanchflower at Dartmouth College, New Hampshire, USA
9. International Labour Office, *Key Indicators of the Labour Market 1999*, London
10. Lois Rogers and Tim Rayment, Stress explosion, *Sunday Times*, 31 December 1995
11. Parents at Work research, London
12. Cary Cooper of UMIST in article (see 10)
13. *Management Today* and WFD research, 1998
14. Penny de Valk, *Price of Success*, Ceridian Performance Partners, 1999
15. Kevin Thomson, *Emotional Capital*, Capstone Publishing, 1998
16. TUC, Report on Bullying in the Workplace, London, 1999
17. CREATE, *Tomorrow's People*, London Human Resource Group.
18. CREATE, *Employability: Bridging the Gap between Rhetoric and Reality*, Centre for Research in Employment and Technology in Europe, 1999
19. Abraham Maslow, *Maslow on Management*, John Wiley & Sons, New York, 1998
20. Ralph Waldo Emerson, quoted by Charles Handy in *The Hungry Spirit*, Random House, London, 1997
21. Jay Conger, Institute of Southern California, in article for *Strategy and Business*, Booz, Allen and Hamilton, USA
22. Charles Handy, *Beyond Certainty: The Changing World of Organisations*, Harvard Business School Press, Boston, MA, USA, 1996
23. Jane Sturges, Birbeck College, Study of 600 graduates in four companies sponsored by Careers Research Forum, UK
24. Andersen Consulting
25. Thoughts for the Millennium
26. Ibid.
27. Mori and WFD, 1999
28. Demos, *Generation X and the New Work Ethic*, London
29. Coopers & Lybrand Research
30. Alvin Toffler, *Powershift: Knowledge, Wealth and Violence at the Edge of the Twenty First Century*, Bantam Books, New York, 1991
31. Margaret Wheatley, *Leadership and the New Science*, Berrett-Koehler, San Francisco, CA, 1992

Chapter 2

1. Warren Bennis, *On Becoming a Leader*, Addison-Wesley, Reading, MA, 1989
2. Daniel Goleman, *Emotional Intelligence*, Bloomsbury, London, 1996
3. Abraham Zaleznik, *The Managerial Mystique*, Harper & Row, New York, 1989
4. Ken Blanchard, Servant leadership revisted, in *Insights on Leadership*, ed. Larry Spears, John Wiley & Sons, New York, 1998
5. Paul Taffinder, *The New Leaders*, Kogan Page, London, 1995
6. Joseph Jaworski, *Synchronicity: The Inner Path of Leadership*, Berrett-Koehler, San Francisco, CA, 1996
7. Sara Melendez, An 'outsider's' view of leadership, in *The Leader of the Future*, eds. Francis Hesselbein, Marshall Goldsmith and Richard Beckhard, Jossey Bass, New York, 1996
8. James MacGregor Burns, op. cit.
9. James Kouzes and Barry Posner, *The Leadership Challenge*, Jossey Bass, San Francisco, CA, 1987
10. Michele Darling, A new vision of leadership, in *The Leader's Companion*, ed. J. Thomas Wren, Simon & Schuster, New York, 1995
11. Marshall Sashkin, Visionary leadership, ibid.
12. Tom Peters, Foreword, in Kouzes and Posner, op. cit.
13. Abraham Zaleznik, Managers and leaders: are they different?, *Harvard Business Review*, May/June, 1977
14. Abraham Zaleznik, 1989, op. cit.
15. *Ibid.*
16. Terrance Powderly, Grand master workman, United States knights of labor 1889, quoted by Alan Briskin, op. cit.
17. Alan Briskin, op. cit.
18. *Ibid.*
19. Richard Sennett, *Authority*, Knopf, New York, 1980
20. Abraham Zaleznik, 1989, op. cit.
21. Joseph Badoracco
22. Margaret Wheatley, op. cit.
23. Alan Briskin, op. cit.
24. James Champey, *Reengineering Management: The Mandate for New Leadership*, Harper Business, New York, 1995
25. James MacGregor Burns, op. cit.
26. Joseph Jaworski, op. cit.
27. Sally Helgesen, *The Web of Inclusion*, Bantam Doubleday, New York, 1995
28. Kouzes and Posner, op. cit.
29. Sara Melendez, op. cit.
30. Margaret Lulic, *Who We Could Be at Work*, Butterworth Heineman, Oxford, 1996
31. Joseph Jaworski, op. cit.
32. Tom Peters and Robert Waterman, *In Search of Excellence*, Harper & Row, New York, 1982

33. Kouzes and Posner, op. cit.
34. Bernard Bass, Concepts of leadership: the beginnings, in *The Leader's Companion*, ed. J. Thomas Wren, Simon & Schuster, New York, 1995
35. *Ancient Egyptian Literature*, vol 1, Ch. 9, Concepts of Leadership: the beginnings by Bernard Bass in *The Healers Companion*, ed. Thomas Wren, Simon and Schuster Inc., New York, 1995
36. Confucius, as quoted in *Great Thinkers of the Eastern World*, ed. Ian P. McGreal, HarperCollins, London, 1995
37. Lao-tzu, from *The Tao of Leadership*, John Heider, Himanics, Atlanta, GA, 1985
38. *Ibid*.
39. Plato, *The Republic*
40. Aristotle, *A Treatise on Government*
41. Professor W.O. Jenkins, 1940, quoted on a leadership programme
42. Mahen Tampoe, ed., *Liberating Leadership*, The Industrial Society, London, 1998
43. Peter Block, *Stewardship*, Berrett-Koehler, San Francisco, CA, 1993
44. John J. Gardner, Quiet presence: the holy ground of leadership, in *Insights on Leadership*, ed. Larry Spears, John Wiley & Sons, New York, 1998
45. Sally Helgesen, Leading from grass roots, in *The Leader of the Future*, Drucker Foundation
46. Francis Hesselbein, The 'how to be' leader, in *The Leader of the Future*, Drucker Foundation
47. James Bolt, Developing three-dimensional leaders, in *The Leader of the Future*, Drucker Foundation
48. Lynne Twist, The Hunger Project, in *The Heart of Service*
49. Joseph Jaworski, op. cit.
50. David Bohm, quoted in Joseph Jaworski, op. cit.
51. Stephen Bergman and Janet Surrey, quoted in John J. Gardner, op. cit.
52. Sally Helgesen, op. cit.
53. *Ibid*.
54. *Henry V* III.i.25–34.
55. Maturana and Varela, quoted by Fritjof Capra in *The Web of Life*, HarperCollins, London, 1996
56. Hermann Hesse, quoted in John J. Gardner, op. cit.

Chapter 3

1. Warren Bennis, *On Becoming A Leader*, Addison-Wesley, Reading, MA, 1989
2. Kouzes and Posner, op. cit.
3. Susan Jeffers, *End the Struggle and Dance with Life*, Hodder and Stoughton, London, 1996
4. Stephen Covey, Foreword, Servant leadership from the inside out, in *Insights on Leadership*, ed. Larry Spears, John Wiley & Sons, New York, 1998
5. Alan Briskin, op. cit.

6. Meister Eckart, quoted by Joseph Jaworski, op. cit.

7. Kay Gilley, *Leading from the Heart*, Butterworth Heinemann, Oxford, 1997

8. Peter Drucker, story told in Abraham Maslow, op. cit.

9. Kahlil Gibran, *The Prophet*, Pan Books, London, 1991

10. Abraham Maslow, op. cit.

11. Marianne Williamson, *A Return to Love: Reflections on the Principles of a Course in Miracles*, HarperCollins, London, 1996

12. Janet Lowe, *Oprah Winfrey Speaks*, John Wiley & Sons, New York, 1998

13. Julian Sleigh, *Crisis Points: Working through Personal Problems*, Floris Books, Edinburgh, Scotland, 1998

14. *Ibid.*

15. Warren Bennis, op. cit.

16. *Ibid.*

17. John Gardner, op. cit.

18. Kouzes and Posner, op. cit.

19. Anthony De Mello, *Awareness*, HarperCollins, New York, 1997

20. *Ibid.*

21. In conversation with Rebecca Stevens

22. Jim Whittaker, quoted in Kouzes and Posner, op. cit.

23. Julian Sleigh, op. cit.

24. Joseph Badaracco and Richard Ellsworth, *Leadership and the Quest for Integrity*, 1989

25. Kay Gilley, op. cit.

26. *Ibid.*

27. Kouzes and Posner, op. cit.

28. Warren Bennis, op. cit.

29. Margaret Wheatley, What is our work?, in *Insights on Leadership*, ed. Larry Spears, John Wiley & Sons, New York, 1998

30. Anthony De Mello,

31. Danah Zohar, *The Quantum Self*, Bloomsbury, London, 1990

32. *Ibid.*

33. Carl Jung, *The Archetypes and the Collective Unconscious*

34. Edna Gundersen, Madonna in USA today, 3 March 1988 (quoted by Sarah Ban Breathnach in *Something More*, Bantam Books, London, 1998)

35. Kouzes and Posner, op. cit.

36. Robert Fritz, *Corporate Tides*, Berrett-Koehler, San Francisco, CA, 1996

37. Kahlil Gibran, op. cit.

38. Abraham Maslow, op. cit.

39. Margaret Wheatley, 1998, op. cit.

40. Kay Gilley, op. cit.

41. Abraham Maslow, op. cit.

42. *Ibid.*

43. Study by Harvard University, summarized in Abraham Maslow, op. cit.

44. Margaret Lulic, op. cit.

45. John Gardner, op. cit.

46. Kouzes and Posner, op. cit.
47. Jean Piaget's work is described more fully by Arie de Geus in *The Living Company*, Harvard Business School Press, Boston, MA, 1997
48. Arie de Geus, op. cit.
49. Vaclav Havel address to Congress 1990, reported in *Time Magazine*, The revolution has just begun, 5 March 1990
50. Abraham Maslow, op. cit.
51. PR Report from Ligget-Stashower, summarized by Margaret Lulic, op. cit.
52. *Ibid.*
53. Oscar Arias, quoted by Rushworth Kidder, Universal human values: finding an ethical common ground, in *The Leader's Companion*, ed. J. Thomas Wren, Simon & Schuster, New York, 1995
54. *Ibid.*
55. *Ibid.*
56. John Gardner, op. cit.
57. Oprah Winfrey, quoted by Janet Lowe, op. cit.
58. Kouzes and Posner, op. cit.
59. *Ibid.*
60. Margaret Wheatley, 1998, op. cit.
61. Robert Greenleaf, op. cit.

Chapter 4

1. Max De Pree, *Leadership is an Art*, Doubleday, New York, 1989
2. Margaret Lulic, op. cit.
3. Confucius, in *Great Thinkers of the Eastern World*, ed. Ian McGreal, HarperCollins, New York, 1995
4. Jesus, in St Matthew 16:26
5. *Hamlet* I.iii.78
6. Socrates at his trial, quoted from *Historic Speeches*, ed. Brian MacArthur, Penguin, Harmondsworth, 1996
7. Plato's Apology
8. Francis Bacon, quoted by Fritjof Capra in *The Turning Point*, Wildwood House, London, 1982
9. *Ibid.*
10. *Ibid.*
11. Margaret Wheatley, 1992, op. cit.
12. Danah Zohar, op. cit.
13. Brian Silver, *The Ascent of Science*, Oxford University Press, Oxford, 1998
14. William Blake, A divine image
15. Quoted by Fritjof Capra, 1996, op. cit.
16. Albert Einstein, Autobiographical notes, in *The World Treasury of Physics*,

Astromony and Mathematics, ed. Timothy Ferris, Little, Brown and Company, 1991

17. Werner Heisenburg, *Physics and Philosophy*, Harper & Row, London, 1962
18. Karl Popper in Schlipp 1974
19. Thomas Kuhn, *The Structure of Scientific Revolutions*, 1962
20. *Ibid.*
21. *Ibid.*
22. *Ibid.*
23. Talcott Parsons, *The Structure of Social Action*, Allen & Unwin, London, 1949
24. Thoman Kuhn, op. cit.
25. Karl Mannheim, *Ideology and Utopia*, Routledge and Kegan Paul, London, 1936
26. Ludwig Wittgenstein, *Tractatus Logico-Philosophicus*, Kegan Paul, London, 1923
27. Xenophanes, in Karl Popper, *The Logic of Scientific Discovery*, Hutchinson, London, 1959
28. Vladimir Nabokov, *Ultima Thule*
29. Fritjof Capra, op. cit.
30. *Ibid.*
31. Peter Checkland, *Systems Thinking, Systems Practice*, John Wiley & Sons, New York, 1981
32. David Bohm, *Wholeness and Implicate Order*, Routledge and Kegan Paul, London, 1980
33. Margaret Lulic, op. cit.
34. Peter Senge, *The Fifth Discipline*, Doubleday, New York, 1990

Chapter 5

1. James MacGregor Burns, op. cit.
2. Richard Hughes, Robert Ginnett and Gordon Curphy, What is leadership?, in *The Leader's Companion*, ed. J. Thomas Wren, Simon & Schuster, New York, 1995
3. Russell Baker, quoted in Kouzes and Posner, op. cit.
4. Mary Parker Follett, *Prophet of Management*, ed. Pauline Graham, Harvard Business School Press, Cambridge, MA, 1995
5. Brian Dumaine, *Fortune Magazine*, 26 December 1994
6. Deming quotation used by his practitioners, Deming Association
7. Nelson Mandela, *Long Walk to Freedom*, Little, Brown and Company, 1994
8. Margaret Lulic, op. cit.
9. Robert Greenleaf, op. cit.
10. Peter Senge, op. cit.
11. Nora Watson, quoted by Studs Turkel in *Working*, 1974
12. Margaret Lulic, op. cit.
13. Robert Greenleaf, op. cit.
14. Dalai Lama

15. Adam Michnik
16. Carol Adrienne, *The Purpose of your Life*, HarperCollins, London, 1998
17. Deepak Chopra, *The Seven Spiritual Laws of Success*, Transworld, London, 1996
18. Alan Briskin, op. cit.
19. Mihaly Csikszentmihalyi, quoted by Carol Adrienne, op. cit.
20. Joseph Jaworski, op. cit.
21. Goethe, quoted by Lulic, op. cit.
22. Ralph Blum, *The Book of Runes*, quoted by Barbara Shipka in *Leadership in a Challenging World*, Butterworth Heinemann, Oxford, 1997
23. United Nations Report 1999
24. National Institute of Economic and Social Research
25. Mother Teresa
26. George Bernard Shaw
27. Kouzes and Posner, op. cit.

Chapter 6

1. Peter Townsend
2. United Nations, Human Development Report, 1997
3. David Korten, *When Corporations Rule the World*
4. Peter Wickens in *The Ascendent Organisation*, Macmillan, London, 1995
5. Thomas Stewart, *Intellectual Capital*, Nicholas Brealey, London, 1997
6. James MacGregor Burns, op. cit.
7. Warren Bennis, The leadership advantage, *Executive Forum*, Spring, 1999
8. Ben Okri, *Mental Fight*, Orion Publishing, London, 1999
9. Gary Zukav, *The Seat of the Soul*, Simon & Schuster, New York, 1990
10. Ben Okri, op. cit.
11. Mary Parker Follett, op. cit.
12. Alvin Toffler, op. cit.
13. Charles Handy, op. cit.
14. Carl Jung, op. cit.

Index